William J. Fay

GOD WITH US

GOD
WITH
US

---

*A Pastoral Theology
of Matthew's Gospel*

MARK ALLAN POWELL

Fortress Press • *Minneapolis*

For David Allen Powell

GOD WITH US
A Pastoral Theology of Matthew's Gospel

Cover design: Peggy Lauritsen Design Group

Library of Congress Cataloging-in-Publication Data

Powell, Mark Allan, 1953–
    God with us : a pastoral theology of Matthew's gospel / Mark Allan
Powell.
        p.   cm.
    Includes bibliographical references and index.
    ISBN 0-8006-2881-0 (alk. paper)
    1. Bible.   N.T.   Matthew—Criticism, interpretation, etc.
    2. Pastoral theology—Biblical teaching.   I. Title.
    BS2575.2.P68   1995
    226.2'06—dc20   95-3448
                                                                             CIP

The paper used in this publication meets the minimum requirements of American National Standard for Information Sciences—Permanence of Paper for Printed Library Materials, ANSI Z329.48-1984.   ∞™

Manufactured in the U.S.A.   AF 1-2881

99   98   97   96   95   1   2   3   4   5   6   7   8   9   10

CONTENTS

ABBREVIATIONS

AB	Anchor Bible	GBS	Guides to Biblical
ABD	*Anchor Bible*		Scholarship
	Dictionary	GNS	Good News
AnBib	Analecta biblica		Studies
AUSS	*Andrews University*	*HBT*	*Horizons in Biblical*
	Seminary Studies		*Theology*
BEvT	Beiträge zur	ICC	International
	evangelischen		Critical
	Theologie		Commentary
Bhy	*Biblebhashyam*	*Int*	*Interpretation*
Bib	*Biblica*	*ITS*	*Indian Theological*
BU	Biblische		*Studies*
	Untersuchungen	*JBL*	*Journal of Biblical*
CBQ	*Catholic Biblical*		*Literature*
	Quarterly	*JRT*	*Journal of Religious*
CC	Continental		*Thought*
	Commentaries	*JSNT*	*Journal for the*
ChL	*Christianity in*		*Study of the New*
	Literature		*Testament*
CTR	*Criswell Theological*	JSNTSS	Journal for the
	Review		Study of the New
EDNT	*Exegetical*		Testament—
	Dictionary of the		Supplement Series
	New Testament	LTPM	Louvain
ESW	Ecumenical		Theological and
	Studies in		Pastoral
	Worship		Monographs
FilN	*Filologia*	*LQ*	*Lutheran Quarterly*
	Neotestamentaria	LXX	Septuagint

NCB	New Century Bible	SBLMS	SBL Monograph Series
NovT	Novum Testamentum	SBT	Studies in Biblical Theology
NovTSup	Novum Testamentum, Supplements	*ScEs*	*Science et esprit*
NTD	Das Neue Testament Deutsch	SNTSMS	Society for New Testament Studies Monograph Series
NTL	New Testament Library	SP	Sacra Pagina
		StP	Studia Pohl
NTM	New Testament Message	*TDNT*	*Theological Dictionary of the New Testament*
NTS	*New Testament Studies*	THKNT	Theologischer Handkommentar zum Neuen Testament
OBT	Overtures to Biblical Theology	TI	Theological Inquiries
PEQ	*Palestine Exploration Quarterly*	*TS*	*Theological Studies*
		WUNT	Wissenschaftliche Untersuchungen zum Neuen Testament
REJ	*Revue des études juives*		
RHPR	*Revue d'histoire et de philosophie religieuses*	*ZNW*	*Zeitschrift für die neutestamentliche Wissenschaft*
RPW	*Reformed and Presbyterian World*	*ZTK*	*Zeitschrift für Theologie und Kirche*
SBL	Society of Biblical Literature		
SBLDS	Society of Biblical Literature Dissertation Series		

PREFACE

THE BASIC IDEA BEHIND THIS BOOK is to approach the theology of Matthew's Gospel through categories related to pastoral theology rather than through categories related to systematic theology (Christology, ecclesiology, eschatology, ethics, salvation history, and so on). Since the latter approach is the one usually taken, my hope is that examining Matthew from a different perspective will yield new insights. This is not to say that the traditional categories are ignored. As it turns out, addressing such topics as worship, mission, and stewardship inevitably involves discussions of Christology, eschatology, and ethics.

The question, perhaps, is which discussion should be the starting point. Are Matthew's beliefs concerning social justice the outworking of a basic ecclesiology, or is Matthew's understanding of the church developed in response to a pastoral concern for justice in society? But such a question may pose a false dichotomy, for I am convinced the process is reciprocal. Pastoral concerns provide the impetus for development of what we would call dogma and affect that development, but pastoral concerns are also addressed from a stance that presupposes prior doctrinal commitments and assumptions. My contribution, then, is intended to supplement rather than replace more traditional studies of Matthean theology.

By "Matthew" I mean not the evangelist but the book that bears this name. This book probably has a complex compositional history; some of the ideas that it presents come from Jesus, while others may come from Mark, from Q, from members of the Matthean community, or from the work's final redactor (the person we usually identify as "Matthew"). But I am interested in the sum of all the ideas presented here and in the overall perspective that their interaction produces. I am attempting to articulate the theology of "The Gospel according to Matthew" or, in literary-critical terms, the theology of the "implied author" of this work. The method of inquiry employed here draws upon modern literary theory but is largely congruent with what has been called composition criticism in the history of exegesis.

Some may find this book appealing or useful simply because it provides Bible studies on five topics relevant for Christian ministry. I have no objection to the book being read from this viewpoint and, in fact, have tried to write it in such a way that the chapters may be consulted independently of each other. I do hope, however, that readers will keep in mind the overriding goal of getting a grasp on Matthew's theology as a whole. I also know that more can and must be done before this goal is fully realized.

To those who use the book to inform their understanding of Christian ministry today I wish to offer one word of pastoral advice of my own. I attempt here to describe the perspective of only one biblical book, the Gospel of Matthew. Although the teaching of Matthew on any given subject may be "biblical," it does not represent "the biblical view" on any subject. With regard to every topic addressed in this volume, other books of the Bible offer additional insights, some of which may challenge or complete understandings derived solely from Matthew.

Since this book often touches on subjects that are controversial in contemporary ecclesial circles, I have endeavored to present a descriptive account of the Matthean perspective that is as free as possible from the influence of my own beliefs and concerns. I recognize, of course, that the myth of "disinterested scholarship" is all but dead in academic circles. The very choice of topics for the chapters reveals some prejudice on my part regarding what is significant for theological understanding, and the mode of approaching each topic also predetermines results in subtle ways. Still, in a sense analogous to what I think Matthew believes about Christian perfection, objectivity in scholarship remains a worthy goal even if its actual attainment is unlikely.

I wish to express my appreciation to Marshall Johnson and others at Fortress Press for bringing this book to publication. Trinity Lutheran Seminary continues to uphold its reputation for unflagging commitment to theological scholarship by encouraging my colleagues and me to produce works such as this and by providing the resources to do so. The first two chapters were originally presented as lectures at the 1993 Ministry Institute sponsored by Trinity Lutheran Seminary, and portions of all five chapters were presented as lectures at the 1993 Great Lakes Theological Academy and the 1993 Wittenberg Pastors' Convocation, both sponsored by the Evangelical Lutheran Church in America's Region VI Center for Continuing Education.

Finally, we owe our greatest debt of gratitude to Melissa C. Curtis, Secretary to the Faculty at Trinity Lutheran Seminary, for typing and correcting the entire manuscript and preparing the indexes.

CHAPTER ONE

MISSION

WHEN WE SPEAK OF MISSION in the Gospel of Matthew,[1] we may describe either the mission of Jesus or the mission of the church that is composed of his followers. Most of the Gospel narrative is devoted to telling the story of Jesus' mission on earth. We learn the divine purpose behind his coming and witness how this purpose is fulfilled in his life, ministry, death, and resurrection. But intertwined with this story of Jesus' mission is material that speaks of the mission to be conducted by Jesus' followers in a place and time beyond the setting of Matthew's story. Much of this material consists of sayings ostensibly directed by Jesus to his disciples, who are major characters in the story. The narrative comes to a close, however, without the disciples having fulfilled the mission directives that Jesus has given them. They have not preached the good news of the kingdom throughout the whole world (24:14); they have not yet preached it anywhere.[2] They have not made disciples of all nations (28:19); they have not yet

---

1. On this subject, see Mortimer Arias and Alan Johnson, *The Great Commission: Biblical Models for Evangelism* (Nashville: Abingdon Press, 1992), 15–34; Donald H. Juel, "Making Disciples: The Mission of the Church in the Gospel according to Matthew," in *Bible and Mission: Biblical Foundations and Working Models for Congregational Ministry*, ed. Wayne Stumme (Minneapolis: Augsburg Publishing House, 1986), 75–86; and Donald Senior, "The Mission Theology of Matthew," in *The Biblical Foundations for Mission*, by Donald Senior and Carroll Stuhlmueller (Maryknoll, N.Y.: Orbis Books, 1983), 233–54.

2. In Matthew's narrative, the disciples are "sent out" by Jesus (10:5a) with instructions for mission (10:5a-42) but are never actually described as conducting the mission with which they have been charged. Whereas Mark and Luke both conclude their accounts of the mission charge with references to the disciples' ministry (Mark 6:12-13; Luke 9:6; 10:17), Matthew concludes his with a reference to the continuing ministry of Jesus (11:1). For one explanation of this

made any disciples at all.[3] They have not even begun to "fish for people," to perform the task that Jesus said would be theirs when he first called them (4:19).

In short, Matthew's narrative ends in a way that seems complete in one sense and yet unfinished in another. This is because the Gospel of Matthew tells the story of Jesus' mission on earth while simultaneously providing the material for another story that could also be told—the story of the mission to be carried out by Jesus' disciples and by people like them, people whom Jesus refers to (in Matthew's Gospel only) as "the church" (16:18; 18:17). Unlike Luke, Matthew does not provide a narrative of this second story. By leaving the story of the church's mission untold, he invites his readers to imagine themselves as participants in the ensuing drama and to consider the role they will play in fulfillment of the church's mission.[4] The literary effectiveness of this approach transcends its inevitable tendency toward historical anachronism.

If we can distinguish between the mission of Jesus and the mission of the church in Matthew, we can also see that the two are closely related. The church is built by Jesus (16:18), and its mission is grounded in his authority (28:18). Jesus promises that he will remain present with those who go out in mission (28:20). Both Jesus (4:16) and his followers (5:14) are described as "light," and both Jesus (2:6) and his followers (9:36-38) fill the role of "shepherds."

Although it is useful to speak of the mission of Jesus and the mission of the church, we might just as well describe these phenomena as "the mission of the earthly Jesus" and "the mission of the exalted Jesus."[5] The mission of the church is actually a con-

---

anomaly, see Dorothy Jean Weaver, *Matthew's Missionary Discourse: A Literary-Critical Analysis* (JSNTSS 38; Sheffield: JSOT Press, 1990), esp. 124–26.

3. Joseph of Arimathea has been made a disciple (*emathēteuthē*), but we do not know by whom (27:57).

4. Many signals in Matthew's narrative indicate that the readers are expected to identify with Jesus' disciples. For example, when the narrator interrupts a speech Jesus is making to his disciples to speak directly to the readers (24:15), the assumption is that the readers are empathizing with the disciples at this point and applying Jesus' words to their own situation. See Mark Allan Powell, *What Is Narrative Criticism?* (GBS; Minneapolis: Fortress Press, 1990), 56–57.

5. Jack Kingsbury describes Matthew's scheme of salvation history as consisting of two epochs: a time of Israel and a time of Jesus (earthly/exalted).

tinuation of the mission of Jesus, conducted by the one who now sits at the right hand of God (26:64). Thus, Jesus can tell his emissaries, "Whoever welcomes you welcomes me" (10:40a). In another sense, both the mission of Jesus and that of the church may be construed as two phases of what is actually the mission of God. Jesus goes on to say, "Whoever welcomes me welcomes the one who sent me" (10:40b).

Our central thesis, then, is that the mission of the church is, for Matthew, a continuation of what God has begun to accomplish in the mission of Jesus on earth. If this is true, then we would expect descriptions of the church's mission in Matthew to resemble descriptions of Jesus' mission in Matthew. This is the case, as the accompanying chart on p. 4 indicates.

THE MISSION OF JESUS

The mission of Jesus is summarized in Matthew's Gospel as being to "save his people from their sins" (1:21). Early in the narrative, we are told that he is given the name Jesus because this is what he will do.[6] Explicit etymologies are usually significant for characterization in literature, and the semantic causality ascribed to the proper name Jesus in Matthew 1:21 is no exception. In literary-critical terms, the intrusive comment of the narrator in this verse establishes the frame of representation within which the character of Jesus is to be understood in the narrative that follows. Or, to borrow structuralist terminology, we may say that in Matthew's narrative the proper name Jesus functions as a *signifier* for which salvation from sins is the *signified*. Thus every recurrence of the proper name Jesus throughout the narrative (150 times)[7] serves as a subtle reminder to the readers that this is the

---

The latter era includes the time of the church. See Jack Dean Kingsbury, *Matthew: Structure, Christology, Kingdom* (Minneapolis: Fortress Press, 1975), 25–36.

6. Since the word "Jesus" literally means "Yahweh saves" or "Yahweh is salvation," the implication of Matt. 1:21 is that God will actually be the one who saves people from sins but that Jesus will be the agent through whom God does this.

7. The number is approximate, depending on acceptance of textual variants. See Fred W. Burnett, "The Undecidability of the Proper Name 'Jesus,' " *Semeia* 54 (1992): 123–44, esp. 137 n. 2.

MISSION IN MATTHEW

The Mission of Jesus	The Mission of the Church
To save his people from their sins (1:21)	To bear fruit (13:23; 21:43)

The Eschatological Character	*The Eschatological Character*
To preach the gospel of the kingdom (4:17, 23; 9:35)	To preach the gospel of the kingdom (10:7; 24:14)
To forgive sins (9:6; 26:28)	To forgive sins (6:11; 18:21-25)
To plunder the house of Satan (12:29)	To overcome the gates of Hades (16:18)
To die on the cross for the sake of many (20:28; 26:28)	To carry the cross in self-denial (16:24)
To be raised from the dead (16:21; 17:9, 23; 20:19)	To tell people Jesus has been raised from the dead (27:64)

The Ethical Dimension	*The Ethical Dimension*
To fulfill the law and the prophets (5:17)	To do the will of God (12:49-50)
by living as a servant (20:28),	by living as servants (20:25-26),
by interpreting the law with authority (5:21-48; 7:28-29).	by binding and loosing with authority (16:19; 18:18).

A Communal Focus	*A Communal Focus*
To build the church (16:18)	To increase the church (13:23)
by making disciples (4:18-22; 9:9; 10:1-4),	by making disciples (28:19),
by calling sinners (9:9-13),	by seeking sinners (18:12-17),
by revealing the Father (11:27).	by confessing the Son (10:32-33).

person who has come to save his people from their sins. But as Jacques Derrida would remind us,[8] every signified tends quickly to become itself a signifier. In other words, as soon as we have established that Jesus' mission is to save his people from their sins, we will have to ask, Who are his people? What are their sins? and, How will he save them?

When Matthew defines Jesus' mission as being to save *his people* from their sins, an important qualification is placed on that mission. Jesus' mission is not to save all people or humankind in general but, specifically, those who can be described as "his people." Still, Matthew's narrative leads us to believe that this is an inclusive category. His people comprise "the lost sheep of the house of Israel" to whom Jesus is initially sent (15:24) as well as some among the "world" (24:14) where the gospel is to be preached (24:14) and the "nations" where disciples are to be made (28:19). His people include the "few" who find the way to life (7:14) and the "many" for whom Jesus gives his life (20:28) and sheds his blood (26:28). His people include the "sinners" whom he has come to call (9:13) and the "righteous" for whom God's kingdom has been prepared (13:43; 25:34). Jesus' people[9] are also referred to as "children of the kingdom" (13:38),[10] "disciples" (28:19), "the elect" (24:22), and "little ones" (10:42; 18:6, 10, 14).

A broader designation that transcends these categories is "the church" (16:18; 18:17). In general, the people whom Jesus has come to save from their sins may be identified with the church, but in making such an identification, we need to keep two points in mind. First, such an identification does not mean that only those who are part of the church will enter the kingdom of heaven. According to Matthew's Gospel, God's kingdom has been prepared for "the righteous" (13:43; 25:34, 37) and anyone who obeys God's commandments may enter the kingdom and

8. See, e.g., Jacques Derrida, *Writing and Difference*, trans. Alan Bass (Chicago: University of Chicago Press, 1978).

9. Grammatically, *autou* in 1:21 refers most naturally to Jesus, not, as is sometimes thought, to God.

10. The people called "children of the kingdom" in 8:12 must be distinguished from those so designated in 13:38.

6 God With Us

find eternal life (5:17; 19:17; 25:46).[11] Thus, figures from Israel's past will be present in the kingdom (8:11), as will some outside the church who have served Jesus unknowingly (25:31-40).[12] Second, Matthew grants that some within the church will not be saved from their sins (18:15-17), since not everyone who calls Jesus "Lord" is known by him (7:21-23). In the world of Matthew's story, wolves can look a lot like sheep (7:15) and experienced field hands have difficulty distinguishing tares from wheat (13:29). Disciples may turn out to be traitors (26:14-16), and even the elect might be led astray (24:24). Accordingly, we do better to identify the people whom Jesus will save from their sins (1:21) as the *true* church, as those who endure to the end (10:22; 24:13) and show by their fruits that they are his people (7:16-20; 12:33).

When Matthew says that Jesus will save these people *from their sins* a further limitation is placed on the mission of Jesus. In this Gospel, the mission of Jesus is not to save his people from persecution or from political oppression, or from any number of other evils that might derive from the sins of others.[13] Jesus' mission is to save his people from their own sins. We note, further, that Matthew does not present Jesus' mission as being to save people from *sin* but from *sins*. No thought is given here to a universal condition of fallen humanity that must be transcended if

11. Matthew freely acknowledges that some people are righteous (1:19; 5:45; 10:41; 13:17, 43; 25:46), although his Gospel also offers sufficient warnings to any who would style themselves as righteous: one's own imperfections can be hard to detect (7:3-5); even those who excel at keeping the commandments may lack something essential (19:16-22); what appears righteous to others does not necessarily satisfy God (23:27-28). The Pharisees are presented as characters who place themselves among "the righteous" (9:13), when actually their righteousness is insufficient for gaining admission to the kingdom (5:20).
12. I interpret 25:31-46 as portraying the judgment of non-Christian "nations" (cf. 28:19) on the basis of how they have treated Christian missionaries (Jesus' siblings). See O. Lamar Cope, "Matthew xxv: 31-46: The Sheep and the Goats Reinterpreted," *NovT* 11 (1969): 32–41; and Graham N. Stanton, *A Gospel for a New People: Studies in Matthew* (Edinburgh: T. & T. Clark, 1992), 207–31. Also, see my comments in chapter 5 below, pp. 113–14, 146–48.
13. Sometimes, though, Jesus does save people from such worldly evils as disease (9:21-22) and storm (8:25).

humans are to enjoy fellowship with God. The concern, rather, is with individual offenses by which people violate the will of God.

Specific examples of such sins are rarely provided within Matthew's narrative. We are not told what sins the people who come to John the Baptist must confess (3:6) or what sins the paralytic must be forgiven (9:2). Still, from the overall context of Matthew's story we learn that people violate God's will when they do what is lawless (7:23; 13:41) or fail to do what God desires (7:21; 12:50). Even actions that are ostensibly good will not meet with God's favor if the motivation for such actions is wrong (6:1-6, 16-18). Speech (5:37; 12:34) and thoughts (9:4) may be evil as well. Accordingly, the sins from which Jesus' people need to be saved are words, actions, thoughts, and attitudes that contravene the will of God.

The effects of such sins are both temporal and eternal. For the present, sins have debilitating consequences that may produce disease (9:2-7). Sins also destroy human community, a point emphasized in Matthew's narrative by the assertion that people sin against each other (18:21; and possibly 18:15, although the text is uncertain). The future consequences of sins are even more dire: alienation from Christ (7:23; 25:12) and an eternal punishment (25:46) that consists of weeping and gnashing of teeth in outer darkness (25:30) or a furnace of fire (13:42).

The mission of Jesus in Matthew's Gospel is to save his people from their sins so that these consequences might be averted. How will he do this? The phrase "salvation from sins" is not defined as such in Matthew's Gospel but is given content through a narrative description of Jesus' activity on earth. When we examine this narrative we discover that Jesus saves his people from their sins in three ways: (1) by announcing and effecting the eschatological rule of God so that sins may now be authoritatively forgiven; (2) by fulfilling the law and the prophets so that sins may now be avoided; and (3) by calling sinners into a new community where the eschatological forgiveness and ethical restraint of sins is a lived reality. Matthew's description of Jesus' mission, then, has an eschatological character, an ethical dimension, and a communal focus.

The Eschatological Character. The mission of Jesus in Matthew's Gospel is fundamentally eschatological.[14] Jesus' ministry includes "preaching the good news of the kingdom" (4:23; 9:35). What does this mean? Although Jesus is said to preach many times, throughout all of Galilee and beyond, the actual content of his sermons is provided only once,[15] when we are offered a one-line summary of the message: "Repent, for the kingdom of heaven has come near" (4:17). This brief assertion is Matthew's representation of the entire preaching career of Jesus, and it is Matthew's definition of "the gospel." The good news concerning the kingdom is the announcement that the kingdom has come near, so near that repentance is both possible and imperative.

The phrases "kingdom of heaven" and "kingdom of God" refer to the reality of God's rule or God's reign,[16] the sphere of influence within which God's will is accomplished. Matthew cannot view the establishment of God's reign as an entirely new reality, since, as the vineyard parable indicates, God's rule has previously been available to Israel (21:33-43). So what does it mean to say that the kingdom of heaven has now "come near"?

---

14. On Matthew's eschatology, see Fred W. Burnett, *The Testament of Jesus-Sophia: A Redaction-Critical Study of the Eschatological Discourse in Matthew* (Washington, D.C.: University Press of America, 1981); Donald A. Hagner, "Apocalyptic Motifs in the Gospel of Matthew: Continuity and Discontinuity," in *HBT* 7/2 (1985): 53–82; idem, "Matthew's Eschatology," in *To Tell the Mystery: Essays on New Testament Eschatology in Honor of Robert H. Gundry*, ed. T. Schmidt and M. Silva (Sheffield: JSOT Press, 1994), 49–71; L. Sabourin, "Traits apocalyptiques dans L'Évangile de Matthieu," *ScEs* 33.3 (1981): 357–72; Günther Bornkamm, "End Expectation and Church in Matthew," in *Tradition and Interpretation in Matthew*, by G. Bornkamm, G. Barth, and H. J. Held, Eng. trans. P. Scott (NTL; Philadelphia: Westminster Press, 1963), 15–51; S. Vadakumpadan, "The Eschatological Perspective in the Gospel of Matthew," *Bhy* 6 (1980): 213–28; and Kathleen Weber, *The Events of the End of the Age in Matthew* (Ph.D. diss., Catholic University of America, 1994). Also look for three papers on Matthew's eschatology by James D. G. Dunn, Robert H. Gundry, and Hans Schwarz in *SBL 1996 Seminar Papers* (Atlanta: Scholars Press, forthcoming).

15. The so-called Sermon on the Mount is no exception, since Matthew characterizes the content of this message as "teaching," not "preaching" (5:2).

16. The Greek word *basileia* is a verbal noun derived from the verb *basileuō*. The traditional English translation "kingdom" is not a verbal noun, as are the English words "rule" and "reign," which most scholars therefore prefer.

From the numerous fulfillment citations scattered throughout this Gospel,[17] we may gather that Matthew views the past history of God and Israel primarily as an era of promise. Matthew knows, for example, that God dwelt with Israel in the Jerusalem temple (23:21), yet Matthew persists in regarding the presence of God among God's people as an ancient promise that has only recently been fulfilled (1:22-23). The coming of Jesus marks the advent of "something greater than the temple" (12:6) such that we may now say "God is with us" (1:23) in a way that God has not been with us before. Similarly, Matthew knows that God has always been "Lord of heaven and earth" (11:25; see also 5:34-35) but believes that God's rule is now being manifested in a way that has been only promised before. What has come near is not simply the transcendent rule of God that has governed all of God's dealings with Israel but, specifically, the eschatological rule of God that brings fulfillment of all God's promises.

Matthew does not represent this establishment of God's reign as now being complete. We must continue to pray for God's kingdom to come and God's will to be done (6:10). But Matthew does portray Jesus as announcing that the final establishment of God's kingdom has begun. The Greek word *ēggiken*, translated "come near" in 4:17, can mean either "soon to arrive" or "already here." For Matthew, the kingdom of heaven announced by Jesus is soon to arrive in its fullness but, in another sense, is already here. Jesus tells the people who witness his exorcisms that they should realize that the kingdom of God has come to them (12:28). Similarly, Jesus speaks of the kingdom as a present reality in Matthew 11:12 ("From the days of John the Baptist until now the kingdom of heaven has suffered violence") and 13:38 ("The field is the world, and the good seed are the children of the kingdom"). To these we might add 21:43 ("The kingdom of God will be taken away from you and given to a people that produces the fruits of the kingdom"), for Matthew's readers are probably expected to regard the prediction Jesus offers here as having already been fulfilled through the establishment of the Christian

17. See esp. 1:22-23; 2:5-6, 15, 17-18, 23; 4:14-16; 8:17; 12:17-21; 13:35; 21:4-5; 26:54, 56; 27:9.

church.[18] Also, the first and the eighth of Matthew's beatitudes (5:3, 10) employ the present tense ("Theirs *is* the kingdom of heaven"), although the other six beatitudes (5:4-9) delineate this current state of blessedness with promises of future reversal ("they *will* be comforted," "they *will* inherit the earth," and so on). Thus Matthew develops a notion of the kingdom that employs what Donald Hagner calls "an altered apocalyptic perspective."[19] The era of fulfillment has begun but is not yet consummated.

In Matthew's vision, the announcement that God's rule has come near constitutes an essential shift in power. Matthew believes that, in some sense, the world has fallen under the rule of the devil. The narrative depicts Satan as the archenemy of Jesus. Like God, Satan has a kingdom (12:26), is served by angels (25:41), and possesses children among the people of the earth (13:38). Satan is able to offer Jesus "all the kingdoms of the world" because they are, or were at the time of that temptation, under his authority (4:8-9).[20] If Jesus had accepted Satan's offer, he may indeed have been granted authority over all these kingdoms, but he would have exercised that authority only as the devil's underling. Jesus opts instead for another role—that of a plunderer. The mission of Jesus according to the Gospel of Matthew is to plunder the devil's house, to take what belongs to Satan and recover what should belong to God (12:29).[21] The conflict is mutual, for from the time John the Baptist first announced the imminence of God's rule (3:2), the kingdom of heaven has been plundered by "the violent" (11:12), that is, by the agents of Satan who try to prevent the word of the kingdom from bearing fruit (13:9). Still, Jesus claims that God has already stepped into history and tied up "the strong" one (12:29), re-

18. Kingsbury, *Matthew: Structure, Christology, Kingdom*, 142.
19. Hagner, "Apocalyptic Motifs," 69.
20. Although Satan's claim to authority is made more explicitly in Luke (4:6) than in Matthew, both Gospels assume that the offer is valid, that Satan really does rule this world. See also John 12:31; 14:30; 16:11; 2 Cor 4:4; Eph 6:12; 1 John 5:19.
21. Jesus is also depicted as coming to recover what is God's in the parable of the rebellious tenants (21:33-41), although here the opposition comes from the religious leaders of Israel.

stricted Satan's apparent free exercise of power. A transfer of authority is taking place. Jesus has been given authority to release people from their sins and from the paralyzing effects that sins produce (9:5-8).

Before Matthew's story is over, Jesus will reveal that he has been given all authority in heaven and on earth (28:16). This announcement comes as the culmination of Matthew's account of Jesus' death and resurrection, which, for Matthew, indicate that the arrival of God's kingdom has passed the point of no return.

Matthew presents the death and resurrection of Jesus as the thing that Satan most wants to prevent (16:21-23), for it is by this that Jesus succeeds in giving his life as a ransom (20:28) and his blood for the forgiveness of sins (26:28).[22] At the moment of Jesus' death, Matthew tells us, "the earth shook, and the rocks were split" (27:51). The event has cosmological significance. "The tombs also were opened, and many bodies of the saints who had fallen asleep were raised. After his resurrection they came out of the tombs and entered the holy city and appeared to many" (27:52-53). Matthew's readers are expected to know that, in the Jewish milieu in which this Gospel was produced, the resuscitation of martyrs was expected to be a sign that the longed-for messianic age had begun (2 Maccabees 7; see also Dan 12:2; Ezek 37:12-14; Zech 14:4-5; 1 Enoch 51:1-5),[23] that God's kingdom was being established at last. For Matthew, then, the death and resurrection of Jesus is an eschatological event that clinches

22. Matthew does not explain *how* Jesus' death brings these benefits. We should not be hasty in ascribing to Matthew a substitutionary view of atonement or presume that Jesus' death is a sacrifice for sin. Some think the resurrection is what gives Jesus universal authority to grant such forgiveness (28:18) and that for Matthew the cross is primarily a means to this end. See Arland Hultgren, *Christ and His Benefits: Christology and Redemption in the New Testament* (Philadelphia: Fortress Press, 1987). But we should not make Matthew a proponent of Christus Victor theory either. Matthew seems content in affirming *that* Jesus' death brings forgiveness of sins without speculating as to how or why it does so.
23. Pheme Perkins, *Resurrection: New Testament Witness and Contemporary Reflection* (Garden City, N.Y.: Doubleday & Co., 1984), 39–47; Paul J. Achtemeier, "An Apocalyptic Shift in Early Christian Tradition: Reflections on Some Canonical Evidence," *CBQ* 45 (1983): 231–48, esp. 241–42; and Dale C. Allison, Jr., *The End of the Ages Has Come: An Early Interpretation of the Passion and Resurrection of Jesus* (Philadelphia: Fortress Press, 1985), 40–46.

what Jesus has announced in his preaching and demonstrated in his ministry: Satan's time of power is passing away and what God wants to happen is beginning to take place.

Matthew's narrative leads us to conclude that Jesus' mission of saving his people from their sins is accomplished in an eschatological sense. Through Jesus' ministry, death, and resurrection the power of Satan is broken. Although the victory will not be finalized until the parousia, the triumph of God's rule over that of the devil means that sins can be forgiven even now (9:2-8; 26:28).

This eschatological conception of salvation is consistent with Matthew's Christology. If Matthew portrays the work of Jesus as the establishment of God's rule, he also describes the person of Jesus as one in whom God is uniquely present (1:23). We noted previously that the etymology for the proper name Jesus provided by the narrator defines the essence of Jesus' mission as being to save his people from their sins (1:21). We may now add that the narrator also gives Jesus an additional name, "Emmanuel," for which an explicit etymology is also provided: "God with us" (1:23). Furthermore, the promise of God's presence inherent in the name Emmanuel is said to be *fulfilled* in the granting of the name Jesus with its new inherent promise of salvation. Significantly, for Matthew the promise of salvation alone, rather than its definitive accomplishment, is sufficient for recognition that God is with us: God is present where there is hope of salvation.

In short, the one through whom God is with us is the one who will save his people from their sins. The logical connection between these two concepts (God's presence and salvation from sins) is clarified when we recognize that Jesus fulfills this mission by establishing God's eschatological rule. One in whom God is present is, by definition, one in whom God's rule is near.

The Ethical Dimension. The mission of Jesus in Matthew's Gospel also has an emphatically ethical dimension, as can be seen by the crisis of decision imposed on people who encounter Jesus in Matthew's narrative (10:34-35; 11:3-6, 20; 12:41; 13:9, 43b).[24] For Matthew, the connection between eschatology and ethics is

24. Kingsbury, *Matthew: Structure, Christology, Kingdom*, 148.

evident in that both present and future dimensions of the reign of God inaugurated by Jesus have ethical ramifications.[25] The imminence of the final judgment makes ethical responsibility imperative, and the curtailing of Satan's power makes righteousness attainable.

Matthew recognizes that "causes of stumbling" (*skandala*) must continue to come (18:7). He also affirms that there have been righteous persons before the coming of Jesus (1:19; 5:10-12; 21:32; 23:35). Thus, his eschatological ethics are neither naive nor novel. As we have seen, Jesus' inauguration of the reign of God affirms that God has, in some sense, been "Lord of heaven and earth" all along (5:34-35; 11:25). In the same way, the ethical dimension of Jesus' mission is an intensification and fulfillment of what has been present already.

Jesus claims that he has come to fulfill the law and the prophets (5:17). Within Matthew's narrative, Jesus is often said to fulfill the prophets when details of his life match quotations from these revered writings.[26] But how does Jesus fulfill the law? He does so in Matthew's narrative in two ways. First, he lives in a way that is perfectly consistent with the will of God. He does this, especially, by living as a servant, as one who has come not to be served but to serve (20:28). His righteousness exceeds that of the scribes and the Pharisees because, unlike them, he does not neglect the weightier matters of the law: justice and mercy and faith (23:23; compare 5:20). Jesus' life and ministry is definitive of justice (12:8), exemplary of mercy (9:13; 12:7), and responsive to faith (8:10; 9:2, 22, 29; 15:28). Second, Jesus fulfills the law in Matthew by authoritatively interpreting the law through his own teaching. Sometimes Jesus' interpretations appear to relax the demands of the law (12:1-8, 9-14), and sometimes they appear to intensify those demands (5:21-48; 19:3-9), but always they are consistent with his recognition that love for God and neighbor are the pinnacle commands from which the law and the prophets hang (22:34-40; compare 7:12). Such an approach lightens the

25. On the intrinsic relationship of eschatology and ethics in the New Testament as a whole, see Wolfgang Schrage, *The Ethics of the New Testament*, trans. David E. Green (Philadelphia: Fortress Press, 1988), 18–39.
26. See n. 17 above.

burdensome demands that the law assumes under other interpreters (23:4), rendering it an easy yoke (11:29-30).

This ethical dimension of Jesus' mission is part of the essentially eschatological mission described above. The fulfillment of
the law and the prophets is one mark of the establishment of
God's reign;[27] it is probably the mark that interests Matthew the
most. The prayer for God's kingdom to come and for God's will
to be done is repetitious parallelism (6:10). The coming of God's
kingdom implies the doing of God's will, for God can only truly
be said to rule when what God wants to happen comes to pass.
We have seen that Jesus' announcement that the kingdom of
heaven has come near is accompanied by a call to repentance
(4:17). The announcement itself discloses an eschatological fact,
and the call to repentance suggests an ethical response. When
people repent, they participate in the establishment of God's rule
by allowing God's will to be done not only on a cosmological
scale but also in their lives.

Ultimately, Jesus' demand that people repent and his ethical
teaching that authoritatively interprets the law serve to fulfill his
mission of saving people from their sins, for only those who do
the will of God will be allowed to enter the kingdom of heaven
(7:21). Furthermore, Jesus' fulfillment of the law and the prophets allows his followers to attain a greater righteousness (5:20) by
which even the temporal effects of sins may be restrained.

A Communal Focus. The mission of Jesus in Matthew's
Gospel also exhibits a focus on community. Jesus does not just go
about teaching, preaching, and healing. He also makes disciples
(4:18-22; 9:9; 10:1-4). The choice of at least one of these disciples
serves as a paradigm for what Jesus claims to be an essential part
of his mission: he has come to call sinners (9:9-13). And Jesus

27. Jewish expectation that the Messiah would come if Israel or a remnant
or representative of Israel would keep the Torah is evident in much literature of
this time. Rabbi Eliezer ben Hyrcanus (ca. 90) puts it negatively in *y. Ta'anit* 1:1:
"If the Israelites do not repent, they will not be redeemed for all eternity."
Rabbi Levi (ca. 300) puts it positively in the Midrash on Song of Solomon 5:2
(118a): "If the Israelites were to repent only for a day, they would be redeemed
at once and the Son of David would come at once." See also *Syriac Baruch* 44:7;
46:5-6.

does not just call such persons as individuals—he also shapes them into a community that he identifies as his family (12:49). His instructions to them concentrate not only on their relationships with him (10:37-38) but also on their relationships with each other (18:15-17; 20:25-27). The mission of Jesus in Matthew's Gospel includes building a church and the foundation for that church is to be found among this community of disciples whom he has called (16:18).

Jesus is able to make disciples and build a church from the sinners whom he calls because as the Son of God he is uniquely qualified to reveal the Father to those whom he chooses (11:27). His disciples are depicted as people of little faith (6:30; 8:26; 14:31; 16:8; 17:20), yet they make the grade with regard to another matter—understanding. In Matthew, the disciples demonstrate a capacity to understand what Jesus tells them (13:51–16:12; 17:13). As people to whom Jesus has revealed the Father, they know the secrets of the kingdom of heaven (13:11). Since they are also people who do the will of God (12:49-50), we might assume that, for Matthew, "hearing and understanding" (13:23) implies "hearing and doing" (7:24).

The community that Jesus' followers represent, then, is an eschatological community that embodies the ethics of repentance. The founding of this community is an essential part of Jesus' mission on earth, for the incorporation of sinners into such a body exemplifies profoundly what is meant by Jesus saving his people from their sins (1:21).

THE MISSION OF THE CHURCH

In Matthew's vision, the establishment of God's reign will not be complete until Jesus returns, coming on the clouds of heaven with power and great glory (24:30; 26:64). When that happens, Satan and his agents will be cast into the eternal fire prepared for them (13:49-50; 25:41).[28] Until then, they will be allowed to remain in this world, like weeds growing among "the children of the kingdom" (13:38).

During this interim, the mission of God begun in Jesus is to continue through the church. The church is in one sense a *corpus*

---

28. See also 3:10, 12; 5:22; 7:19; 13:40; 18:8-9.

mixtum infiltrated by false prophets (7:15; 24:11, 24) and persons unknown to Jesus (7:23; 25:12). Still, it is in the life and mission of the church that Jesus remains present and active in the world (10:40; 18:20; 28:20).[29]

Matthew's understanding of the mission of the church is summarized in the phrase "to bear fruit." In a basic sense, "to bear fruit" means simply to reproduce that which has been sown. Grapes are not gathered from thorns, nor figs from thistles (7:16). The church's role, then, is not to be innovative but to produce the fruit that Jesus' mission on earth will inevitably bear.

How is the church to do this? When we examine the narrative of Matthew's Gospel more closely, we find that the metaphor of fruit bearing is used in a threefold sense. To bear fruit means (1) to respond appropriately to the coming of God's eschatological rule and to participate in its establishment; (2) to exhibit the ethics of the kingdom that are the qualitative sign by which God's people are known; and (3) to contribute to the numerical increase of the eschatological community that embodies these ethics. Like the mission of Jesus, then, the mission of the church in Matthew has an eschatological character, an ethical dimension, and a communal focus.

The Eschatological Character.   In Matthew, the metaphor of fruit bearing is itself eschatological. The seed that produces such fruit (when it falls on good soil) is identified in Matthew not simply as "the word" (Mark 4:14) or even as "the word of God" (Luke 8:11) but as "the word of the kingdom" (Matt 13:19). To prevent this seed from bearing fruit is now the principal aim of the evil one (13:19). In Matthew's vision, the eschatological clash of cosmic powers has come to this: the children of the kingdom must grow among weeds sown by the devil (13:38-39). The ultimate question is, Will the seed sown by Jesus bear fruit in the life and ministry of the church?

29. The identification of Jesus with the least of his siblings in 25:31-46 is also meant to affirm his presence in the church. The hungry, thirsty, estranged, naked, sick, and imprisoned persons with whom he is present are followers of Christ who become needy when they answer his call to take the gospel to the nations (cf. 10:8-15, 40-42). See Stanton, *Gospel for a New People*, 207–31.

Jesus tells the religious leaders of Israel that the kingdom of God will be taken away from them and given to people who will produce the fruits of it (21:43; compare 21:34, 41). For Matthew, the church has superseded Israel as the eschatological people of God[30] and the church's primary task as the eschatological people of God is to produce the fruits of the kingdom that God desires. How does the church do this? It does so largely by continuing to do what Jesus has done. If Jesus preached "the good news of the kingdom" throughout all Galilee (4:23), his followers will preach "the good news of the kingdom" throughout the whole world (24:14). When Jesus' disciples preach, the content of their sermons is to be summarized in the same words used for Jesus' own message: "The kingdom of heaven has come near" (10:7).[31]

For Matthew, the soteriological significance of Jesus' eschatological announcement is that by his life, death, and resurrection Jesus receives authority to forgive sins (9:9; 20:28). The church is expected to continue proclaiming and practicing the radical forgiveness of sins initiated by Jesus. Followers of Jesus will forgive each other not only seven times but seventy times seven (18:21-22). In the parable of the Unforgiving Servant (18:23-35), we learn that God's forgiveness of enormous human debts provides the model for God's people in settling accounts with each other. The church is to remember this link between divine and human forgiveness every time it prays in the manner Jesus taught his followers to pray (6:11).

The church that Jesus builds is expected to overcome "the gates of Hades" (16:18). For Matthew, the term "Hades" describes the sphere of Satan's waning power, with special emphasis on the most noticeable effect of that power, death. The use of the metaphor "gates" implies that the realm where death and the devil rule has now assumed a defensive position. When Jesus says

---

30. Much discussion in Matthean studies has focused on whether the church is potentially inclusive or necessarily exclusive of Israel. Arguments for the latter usually appeal to the charge to make disciples of "the Gentiles" (*ta ethnē*) with which the Gospel concludes (28:19; cf. 10:5). But other passages suggest that Matthew assumes that the church will continue to work within Israel as well (10:23; 23:34).

31. The same message was also proclaimed by John the Baptist as forerunner of Jesus (3:2).

that the gates of Hades will not prevail against his church, he does not mean that the church will be able to withstand the attacks of the devil. Gates do not attack; they get attacked. Jesus expects the church to storm the gates that preserve the last vestiges of the devil's influence, and he promises that those gates will give way before such an assault.[32] The image in Matthew of the church overcoming the gates of Hades is parallel to the image of Jesus plundering Satan's house. Both Jesus and the church are represented as proclaiming the establishment of God's rule and then acting aggressively to claim for God what is God's.

As we have seen, the eschatological mission of Jesus in Matthew also includes giving his life as a ransom and shedding his blood for the forgiveness of sins. This is a unique aspect of Jesus' mission that the church cannot and need not repeat. The church's mission, however, does include bearing testimony to the death of Jesus by mirroring his death in the lives and deaths of his followers.[33] As the church conducts its mission, many of Jesus' followers will suffer the same fate that befell him (10:25). They will be hauled before councils, beaten by religious authorities, and dragged before pagan political rulers just as he was (10:17-18; compare 26:57-59, 67; 27:1-2). Some will have to "drink the cup" that he was to drink, to suffer death in accord with God's will (20:23; 26:39). But whereas Jesus gave his life for the sake of many (20:28; 26:28), his followers give theirs for the sake of one, namely, Jesus himself (10:39; 16:25). To say that Jesus' followers give their lives for his sake implies two things. First, their allegiance to him is what will bring about their deaths (10:22; 24:9). Second, their deaths will serve as a testimony to his, calling attention to what God accomplished through it. Even those who do not suffer death in a literal sense (24:22) may offer such testimony by living lives of self-denial. Those who live in such a way

32. This understanding of Matt 16:18 dates at least to a sixteenth-century commentary by J. Maldonatus, now published as *A Commentary on the Holy Gospels*, 2 vols. (London: Hodges, 1888). See vol. 1, p. 41. Joel Marcus suggests a different image in "The Gates of Hades and the Keys of the Kingdom (Matt 16:18-19)," *CBQ* 50 (1988): 443-55.

33. Curiously, Matthew contains no explicit indication that the church is to testify to Jesus' death through preaching, although this may be assumed to be a part of its proclaiming the resurrection (27:64).

are described metaphorically as taking up their crosses and following Jesus (10:38; 16:24). The choice of such a metaphor indicates that the life of self-denial, like actual martyrdom, testifies to the death of Jesus and its eschatological significance.

The eschatological mission of Jesus culminated in his resurrection from the dead. Jesus' followers who lose their lives for his sake will find eternal life in the age to come (10:39; 16:25; 19:29), but they are not expected to be raised from the dead in this age in any sense analogous to the resurrection of Jesus.[34] Again, since the church cannot and need not duplicate this component of Jesus' mission, its role consists of proclaiming what Jesus has done. Matthew illustrates this dramatically in an ironic scene near the end of his narrative (27:62-64). The enemies of Jesus believe they have won. Jesus is dead and his followers have forsaken him and fled. Still, they are worried about one thing. What if Jesus' followers began to tell people that he has been raised from the dead? If this were to happen, they imagine, they would be worse off than if they had never had him crucified in the first place. The irony in this story is that those who fear preaching of the resurrection have not yet reckoned with the possibility that Jesus might really rise from the dead. What troubles them is the prospect that Jesus' disciples might steal his body and perpetrate rumors of a resurrection. If the proclamation of a false resurrection is threatening to Satan's agents,[35] then how much more devastating will the preaching of the true resurrection turn out to be!

In short, the mission of the church duplicates that of Jesus in terms of its proclamation of the good news that the kingdom is near and in terms of its actualization of this good news through the overcoming of Satan's strongholds on earth. The mission of the church also supplements that of Jesus by demonstrating the significance of Jesus' unique death and resurrection through

34. The resuscitation of the saints reported in 27:52-53 does not contravene this point, for there is no indication that they, like Jesus, have risen no more to die. The resurrection of Jesus is unique in that only he remains eternally present after his resurrection (28:20).

35. That the religious leaders of Israel are to be regarded as agents of Satan in Matthew's narrative is clear from Jesus' description of them as "evil" (12:34) and as "plants" that the "heavenly Father has not planted" (15:13), both of which mark them as "children of the evil one" (13:38-39).

preaching, self-denial, and martyrdom. By so doing, the church produces "the fruits of the kingdom" (21:43).

We noted above that the eschatological character of Jesus' mission in Matthew is consistent with Matthean Christology: the one in whom God is present is naturally the one through whom God's rule is established. In the same way, the eschatological character of the church's mission is consistent with Matthew's ecclesiology. For this Gospel, the church is the community of people with whom Christ dwells (18:20; 28:20). Since Matthew's narrative portrays God as present in Jesus, and Jesus as present in the church, the mission of the church logically involves active participation in the establishment of God's eschatological rule.

The Ethical Dimension. The eschatological mission of the church, like that of Jesus, has an ethical dimension that receives special emphasis in Matthew. The ministry of Jesus' followers engenders a crisis of decision comparable to that introduced by Jesus himself (10:11-15; 23:34-35).

Just as Jesus' eschatological proclamation included a call to repentance, so the fruit that the church is to bear is "fruit worthy of repentance" (3:8). To bear fruit, then, may mean simply to do the will of God. We have seen that an important part of Jesus' mission, for Matthew, is that he fulfills the law and the prophets in a double sense, by living in a way that is perfectly consistent with God's will and by authoritatively interpreting the law in a way that reveals God's will. The ethical dimension of the church's mission parallels the mission of Jesus in both of these ways.

First, the church is to bear fruit by doing the will of God. Jesus specifically describes his family as consisting of disciples who do the will of God (12:49-50). They are to be perfect, as their heavenly Father is perfect (5:48). The will of God that they are to do, furthermore, is explicated in terms of the servant mentality exemplified by Jesus. Just as the Son of Man came not to be served but to serve, so they are to be servants to each other (20:25-28)— and not only to each other but to the world at large. They are to give to all who beg (5:42) and to love even their enemies (5:44). Doing the will of God means doing "good works." Jesus' followers are the light of the world (5:14). They are to let their light so shine before others that people will see their good works and glorify God (5:15).

The performance of good works is not a peripheral part of the church's eschatological mission for Matthew; rather, it is the very heart of it. We see this in the repeated assertion that a tree is known by its fruits (7:16, 20; 12:33). The good works that Jesus' followers do are the proof that their gospel is of God (7:16). They are the assurance that the rule of God that has taken root in the world will not wither (21:19).

The good works that the church performs include the basic tasks of preaching and healing, which, as we have seen, are the means through which it demonstrates the inauguration of God's rule. When Jesus withdraws into Galilee to begin preaching his eschatological good news of the kingdom, Matthew says that this fulfilled the following prophecy: "The people who sat in darkness have seen a great light, and for those who sat in the region and shadow of death light has dawned" (4:16). Thus, when Jesus says a short while later (5:16) that his disciples let *their* light shine when they do good works, Matthew's readers may be expected to remember that the metaphor of a light shining has been used specifically to describe the preaching of the gospel. Or again, since Jesus' healing of a man with a withered hand is described as a good work in 12:12, the good works enjoined of Jesus' disciples in 5:16 may also be taken to include acts of healing (see 10:8).

The ethical dimension of the church's mission also includes providing authoritative interpretations of God's will. The church does this primarily by teaching people to obey all that Jesus has commanded (28:20). But this does not simply mean that the church is to remember and propagate the interpretations that Jesus gave to various laws. Matthew realizes that the matter is more complicated than that. Jesus' interpretations of Moses' commands have already become commands of Jesus that will themselves require interpreting. So the church is given the authority to "bind and loose" (16:19; 18:18). Binding and loosing are rabbinic expressions for determining the manner in which laws apply to specific situations.[36] An important part of the

36. Günther Bornkamm, "The Authority to 'Bind' and 'Loose' in the Church in Matthew's Gospel: The Problem of Sources in Matthew's Gospel," in *The Interpretation of Matthew*, ed. Graham N. Stanton (Philadelphia: Fortress Press, 1983), 85–97; J. D. M. Derrett, "Binding and Loosing: (Matt 16:19;

church's mission for Matthew is to function as the authoritative
body that determines what is or is not the will of God. In a sense,
then, Matthew may picture followers of Jesus as exercising a role
analogous to that of the scribes and the Pharisees who have offered supposedly authoritative interpretations of the law (but see
7:29). An essential difference for Matthew is that the church will
continue to follow Jesus' hermeneutical lead in interpreting the
entire law and prophets in light of the love commandments
(20:34-40). To teach people to observe all that Jesus has commanded means above all to teach them that love for God and love
for neighbor are the essential requirements of a God who values
mercy more than sacrifice (9:13; 12:7).[37]

In short, the ethical dimension of the church's mission duplicates the mission of Jesus on earth both with regard to keeping
the will of God and with regard to authoritatively interpreting
God's will. As with the mission of Jesus, these aspects of the
church's work derive from the eschatological character of its mission, since the accomplishment of God's will is the fruit that indicates that God's kingdom is being established.

A Communal Focus. The mission of the church also continues the focus on community evident in the mission of Jesus on
earth. An essential part of Jesus' mission was to make disciples
(4:18-22; 9:9; 10:1-4), and the Great Commission given to those
disciples at the end of the narrative is for them to do the same
(28:19). Thus Jesus' final words to his disciples in Matthew's nar-

18:18; John 20:23)," *JBL* 102 (1983): 112–17; and Marcus, "Gates." Dennis C.
Duling lists six different interpretations that have been given to this phrase in
"Binding and Loosing: Matthew 16:19; Matthew 18:18; John 20:23," *Forum* 3,
4 (1987): 3–32, esp. 6–11, and to these may be added a seventh recently pro-
posed by J. Andrew Overman in *Matthew's Gospel and Formative Judaism: The
Social World of the Matthean Community* (Minneapolis: Fortress Press, 1990),
104–6. But usage of the terms *deō* ("bind") and *lyō* ("loose") in Josephus, in tar-
gumic material, and as the likely translations for the Aramaic equivalents of
Hebrew terms in rabbinic writings confirms the majority view that they refer to
determination of what the law allows and forbids. See H. Strack and P. Biller-
beck, *Kommentar zum Neuen Testament aus Talmud und Midrash*, 6 vols. (Munich:
C. H. Beck, 1922–61), 1:732–38; and the excellent article by Raymond F. Collins in *ABD*, 1:743–45.
37. On the ministry of binding and loosing, see below, pp. 67–68, 86–88.

rative reinforce his initial words to them: "I will make you fish for people" (4:19). This aspect of the church's mission may represent an additional nuance of the basic mandate to bear fruit. Bearing fruit is a common biblical metaphor for reproduction (for example, Gen 1:28), and so the disciples of Jesus may bear fruit by reproducing themselves, that is, by making more disciples. This element of numerical increase is stressed in the parable of the Sower, where the seed that falls on good soil is said to bear fruit by yielding thirty, sixty, or even a hundredfold (13:23). Such increase is also displayed parabolically through eschatological images that liken God's kingdom to a plant (13:31-32) or to leaven (13:33) that grows. Since God is Lord of heaven and earth (5:34-35; 11:25), the sphere of God's rule cannot itself expand. The number of people who acknowledge God's rule can increase, however, and this must be what is meant when God's kingdom is described as growing.

Matthew has no illusions about the relative success that the church will experience in its mission of making disciples. Most people prefer the wide and easy way that leads to destruction to the narrow and difficult path to life (7:13-14). And when the good news of the kingdom is proclaimed in this world, more often than not it will fall on unreceptive soil or will be received by those who hear but do not understand (13:18-22; compare 13:15). But every disciple who does hear and understand has the potential for making many more disciples (13:23; 28:19).

The disciples of Jesus are presented in Matthew as people who hear the word and understand (13:51; 16:12; 17:13),[38] people who have ears that hear (13:16; compare 11:15; 13:9, 43). This is what qualifies them for the mission of making disciples of all nations. They are also, as we have seen, people of little faith (6:30; 8:26; 14:31; 16:8; 17:20), but this does not disqualify them from the mission of making disciples of all nations. The world is blessed with people of great faith who may turn up at surprising and unpredictable junctures. Jesus encounters two such persons in his own ministry: a centurion (8:10) and a Canaanite woman

---

38. The author of Matthew's Gospel has apparently redacted the Gospel of Mark to remove references to the disciples' *not* understanding. Compare 14:31; 16:9; 17:9, 23 with Mark 6:52; 8:17; 9:10, 32.

(15:28). But he does not commission either of these individuals to make disciples. Furthermore, although Jesus frequently chides his disciples for their lack of faith, he never offers them any remedy for this inadequacy. Instead of suggesting how they might increase their faith, he assures them that even the tiniest amount of faith will be sufficient (17:20). Even after the resurrection, when their worship is still marred by doubt (28:17; compare 14:31-33), this lapse does not forestall Jesus from commissioning them to make disciples. To fulfill the mission of making disciples, then, understanding is more important than great faith. Likewise, according to Jesus' parable of the Sower, those who bear fruit are not merely ones who receive the word of the kingdom with joy (13:20-21); rather, they are ones who hear the word and understand (13:23).

We can see why this is so when we note the means through which Jesus' followers are to make disciples: by baptizing in the name of the Father, Son, and Holy Spirit, and by teaching people to observe all that Jesus commanded (28:19-20). Baptism, for Matthew, signifies incorporation into the eschatological community created by Jesus. Without crediting this community with developed trinitarian doctrine, we may at least assume from the baptismal formula that it defined itself in terms of its understanding of and relationship to the Father, Son, and Holy Spirit. Jesus' disciples are persons to whom Jesus has revealed the Father (11:27; 13:11, 16-17), and they are also persons to whom the Father has revealed the Son (11:27; 16:16; compare 14:33). The latter is especially significant for fulfillment of the Great Commission. Notably, the church is not commissioned to continue revealing the Father, for this is something that only the Son can do. Jesus' followers are called, however, to confess Jesus before others (10:32-33). To make disciples according to the baptismal formula provided in 28:19, such confession must be acknowledgment of Jesus as the Son of God.

As persons to whom the Father has revealed the Son (11:27), Jesus' disciples know that Jesus is the Son of God (16:16; compare 14:33) and this identification of Jesus as the Son of God is what offers the fundamental justification for baptism in the name of the Father, Son, and Holy Spirit. People who hold Jesus to be simply a prophet, or even the messiah, would never baptize in this way. Appreciation for God as Father and as Holy Spirit is, of course, traditional and commonplace in Judaism. It is not hard to imagine any number of groups who might baptize in the name of either the Father or the Holy Spirit or both. But why would they baptize in the name of the Son unless they believe that God has a Son and that they know who this Son is? In short, the disciples' understanding of Jesus as the Son of God is what qualifies them to make disciples by baptizing in this threefold name.

Jesus' followers are also to make disciples by teaching observance of all that Jesus has commanded. They are qualified to do this because, as we have seen, they are the only characters throughout the narrative who have been said to understand Jesus' teaching (13:51; 16:12; 17:13). It has been given to them to know the secrets of the kingdom of heaven (13:11). Now, in making disciples of all nations, they are to make known to others what they have understood. They are to utter in the light what they have been told in the dark and to proclaim upon the housetops what has been whispered (10:27). What is it that has been covered but will now be revealed, hidden that will now be made known (10:26)? Matthew does not tell us, but we may assume such hidden knowledge to include the revelations that the kingdom of heaven is near (4:17) and that Jesus is the Son of God (16:16).

The commission that Jesus' disciples receive at the end of the narrative, however, lays the emphasis on the ethical ramifications of the eschatological insights just mentioned. They are to teach people *to obey* all that Jesus has *commanded* (28:20). We are reminded at once of the parable of the wise builder who, Jesus says, exemplifies those who hear his words and *do* them (7:24). If Jesus' disciples are to teach all of Jesus' commands, they will surely include his first: "Repent!" (4:17). Making disciples, then, means teaching those who are incorporated into the eschatological community to do the will of God (12:49-50).

In short, the church's mission of making disciples is to be carried out by people who know that Jesus is the Son of God, who understand the eschatological truth that undergirds the church's mission, and who live in a manner consistent with God's will. Such persons will be able to baptize in the name of the Father, Son, and Holy Spirit, and will be able to teach obedience to Jesus' commands even if they are themselves persons of little faith, persons who doubt (28:17).

Just as the mission of Jesus was especially directed to sinners, whom he sought at the expense of ignoring the righteous (9:13), so too will the church's mission be directed especially toward those who have been excluded from traditional religious groupings. Disciples are to be made specifically from "the nations" or Gentiles, who are virtually synonymous with sinners in Matthew's narrative (18:17). The church's mission will also include special concern for the recovery of community members who sin (18:15-17). Concern for the one who has gone astray is to take precedent over concern for the ninety-nine who have not (18:10-14). Ironically, the disciples to whom Jesus directs these words regarding recovery of the lapsed become persons in need of recovery themselves before Matthew's narrative comes to a close (26:56; 28:7).

SUMMARY

The mission of Jesus according to the Gospel of Matthew is to save his people from their sins (1:21). For Matthew, this mission is accomplished in an eschatological sense. By announcing and effecting the establishment of God's reign, Jesus assumes authority formerly claimed by Satan (4:8-9; 12:28-29; 28:18). As a result, Jesus is able to forgive sins and release people from their temporal and eternal consequences (9:1-8; 26:28). Matthew is particularly interested in the ethical dimension of this eschatological salvation by which Jesus brings about the fulfillment of the law and the prophets (5:17). Matthew further emphasizes that this eschatological salvation is realized within the church, the community of sinners called by Jesus. Jesus remains present with the church (18:20; 28:20) and continues to be active through its ministry.

The mission of the church, then, is to bear the fruits of those who have been saved from their sins by Jesus. The fruits that the church are to bear are the eschatological "fruits of the kingdom" (21:43) that grow from the "word of the kingdom" sown by Jesus (13:19). The church produces these fruits by continuing Jesus' mission of proclaiming and demonstrating the imminence of God's rule. Once again, Matthew is particularly interested in the ethical dimension of this mission, for "fruit worthy of repentance" (3:8) becomes the qualitative sign by which the true people of God are identified (7:15-20; 12:33). Finally, the church's mission of bearing fruit also involves a commitment to quantitative increase (13:23) by which new disciples are made (28:19) and the community established by Jesus grows in size and diversity.

The threefold meanings given to "salvation from sins" and "fruit bearing" in Matthew's Gospel allow these concepts to be developed in such a way that the mission of Jesus and the mission of the church are similar. In both cases, the mission is essentially accomplished through the incorporation of people into eschatological communities that embody the ethics of repentance. And in both cases, the theological basis for this mission lies in the belief that God's eschatological rule has been inaugurated through the life, death, and resurrection of Jesus.

CHAPTER TWO

WORSHIP

ALTHOUGH MATTHEW'S GOSPEL is typically regarded as "the Gospel of the church," worship is a less prominent theme in this book than in its Synoptic companion, the Gospel of Luke.[1] The literature on worship in the New Testament in general is vast,[2] but, to my knowledge, no major treatments of this theme *in Matthew* have been produced.[3] This chapter will delineate the words and passages most closely associated with worship in Matthew and will then describe the types, forms, and moods of worship they represent. It will conclude with a general analysis of Matthew's depiction of worshipers, of worship settings, and of worship recipients.

1. Whereas Matthew reports thirteen instances of worship (2:11; 8:2; 9:8, 18; 11:25; 14:33; 15:25, 31; 18:26; 20:20; 21:16; 28:9, 17), Luke reports twenty (1:46, 64; 2:13, 20, 28, 37; 4:15; 5:25, 26; 7:16; 13:13; 17:15, 16; 18:11, 43 (twice); 19:37; 23:47; 24:52 (?), 53). The disparity appears greater in many English Bibles because of a hesitation in translating *proskyneō* in Matthew as "worship" when Jesus is the recipient.
2. Some of the most important include Paul F. Bradshaw, *The Search for the Origins of Christian Worship: Sources and Methods for the Study of Early Liturgy* (New York: Oxford University Press, 1992); Gerhard Delling, *Worship in the New Testament*, trans. Percy Scott (Philadelphia: Westminster Press, 1962); Ferdinand Hahn, *The Worship of the Early Church*, trans. David E. Green (Philadelphia: Fortress Press, 1973); Ralph P. Martin, *Worship in the Early Church* (Grand Rapids: Wm. B. Eerdmans, 1964); C. F. D. Moule, *Worship in the New Testament* (ESW 9; Richmond: John Knox Press, 1961); David Peterson, *Engaging with God: A Biblical Theology of Worship* (Grand Rapids: Wm. B. Eerdmans, 1992); Eduard Schweizer, "Worship in the New Testament," *RPW* 24 (1957): 196–205; and Franklin W. Young, "The Theological Context of New Testament Worship," in *Worship in Scripture and Tradition*, ed. Massey H. Shepherd (New York: Oxford University Press, 1963), 77–97. Oscar Cullmann's classic study, *Early Christian Worship* (London: SCM Press, 1953), is devoted primarily to the Gospel of John.
3. For a recent, brief study, see Peterson, 81–93.

WORD USAGE

We begin with a survey of Matthew's vocabulary for worship,[4] noting how each word is used in Matthew. Comments on translations are based on a survey of nine English versions: Jerusalem Bible (JB), King James Version (KJV), New American Standard Bible (NASB), New English Bible (NEB), New International Version (NIV), New Jerusalem Bible (NJB), New Revised Standard Version (NRSV), Revised English Bible (REB), and Revised Standard Version (RSV).

1. *Ainos* is used only once, in 21:16, a verse unique to Matthew in the New Testament but derived from LXX Ps 8:3. The word is translated "praise" in all versions except the RSV, which prefers "perfect praise." The latter translation is unfortunate, derived from the KJV's rendering of *katartizō* in the same verse as "perfected." As we shall see, the praise referred to in 21:16 is not perfect from a Matthean perspective.

2. *Doxazō* is used three times in Matthean passages that have no parallel (5:16; 6:2; 15:31) and once in a passage found also in Mark and Luke (9:8, par Mark 2:12; Luke 5:26). The word is typically translated as "give glory," "glorify," "praise," or "give praise." The only exception is 6:2, where some versions present the hypocrites in the synagogues as giving alms so that they will "win admiration" (JB, NEB, NJB) or "be honored" (NIV). Such translations fail to convey the Matthean thought that these persons covet for themselves prerogatives that rightly belong to God alone. In fact, with the exception of 6:2, *doxazō* occurs in Matthew only with reference to God; it is not used with reference to Jesus, as in Luke 4:15.[5]

3. *Eulogeō*, typically translated "bless," is not used as a general term for worship in Matthew as it is in Luke (1:64; 2:28; 24:53). Of its five occurrences in Matthew, three are simply adjectival participles that describe persons as "blessed" (21:9, par Mark

---

4. In addition to the relevant *TDNT* entries, see Mark Harding, *The Terminology of Respecting and Serving God in the New Testament Era* (M.A. diss., Sydney: Marquarrie University, 1987); Karen H. Jobes, "Distinguishing the Meaning of Greek Verbs in the Semantic Domain of Worship," *FilN* 4 (1991): 183–91; Moule, 67–81; and Peterson, 55–74.

5. Luke uses *doxazō* for Jesus, but not *proskyneō* (unless the variant at 24:52 is accepted). With both Matthew and Mark, the reverse is true.

11:9, Luke 19:38; 23:39, par Luke 13:35, see Ps 118:26; 25:34). The other two uses refer specifically to the blessing of food for a meal (14:19, par Mark 6:41, Luke 9:16; 26:26, par Mark 14:22). Although this is something that may occur within a worship context, "blessing food" is not a synonym for worship in Matthew in the sense that "blessing God" is in Luke.

4. *Eucharisteō* is also not used as a general term for worship in Matthew as it is in Luke (17:16; 18:11). The word is usually translated "give thanks" and is found only twice in Matthew (15:36, par Mark 8:6; 26:27, par Mark 14:23, Luke 22:17). Once again, both of these references are within the specific context of a table grace. For Matthew, *eulogeō* and *eucharisteō* are synonyms that may be used interchangeably (compare 15:36 with 14:19 and 26:27 with 26:26).

5. *Exomologeomai* is used as a general term for worship only once in Matthew (11:25), in a passage paralleled by Luke 10:21. The word is variously translated as "thank" (KJV, NEB, NRSV, REB), "give thanks" (RSV), "bless" (JB, NJB), and "praise" (NASB, NIV). Matthew also uses the word in a more restricted sense in 3:6 (par Mark 1:5), where it is consistently translated "confess." Here, as in the uses of *eulogeō* in 14:19 and 26:26, the reference is to an activity that might occur within a context of worship but that is not synonymous with worship per se. The root meaning of *exomologeomai* is "to make public acknowledgment." To acknowledge God publicly (11:25) means "to worship" in Matthew 11:25 in the same sense that "to bless God" means "to worship" in Luke (1:64; 2:28; 24:53). But to acknowledge one's sins (3:6) is not definitive of worship any more than is blessing food for a meal.

6. *Latreuō* is used only once, in 4:10, a verse that quotes Deut 6:13 and is paralleled by Luke 4:8. The word is consistently translated "serve," except in the NEB and REB, where it is translated "worship." Luke also uses the word in two unparalleled passages (1:74; 2:37), the latter of which explicates the term as "fasting and prayer." In Matthew 4:10, *latreuō* is used in synonymous parallelism with *proskyneō*.[6]

---

6. For a discussion of *latreuō* in four non-Matthean texts (Phil 3:3; John 4:23-24; Heb 13:15-16; Rom 12:1), see A. Boyd Luter, Jr., " 'Worship' as Service: The New Testament Usage of *Latreuō*," *CTR* 2 (1988): 335–44.

7. *Proskyneō* is used thirteen times in Matthew (2:2, 8, 11; 4:9, 10; 8:2; 9:18; 14:33; 15:25; 18:26; 20:20; 28:9, 17). None of these occurrences is paralleled in Mark, although Mark does use *proskyneō* in two passages where Matthew does not (5:6; 15:19; see Matt 8:28; 27:30). Only two of Matthew's uses are paralleled in Luke (4:9, 10, par Luke 4:7, 8), and Luke elsewhere uses *proskyneō* only in 24:52, which is unparalleled and textually uncertain.

The details of the English translations of Matthew's thirteen uses of this term are too cumbersome for full consideration here, but we should note that of the nine versions surveyed, only the KJV translates *proskyneō* as "worship" consistently. The others vary the translation with regard to context. The word is rendered either "worship" or "do homage" in passages that involve supernatural beings (4:9, 10) and in the references to the baby who is called "king of the Jews" (2:2, 8, 11). But the word is usually translated by "kneel," "bow," or an equivalent expression in passages that involve encounters between human beings. Some versions, however, revert to using "worship" or "do homage" in references to the risen Jesus (28:9, 17) and a few also do so in 14:33 where Jesus is confessed to be the Son of God. Such careful distinctions in translation are unnecessary, for, as we shall see, all thirteen uses of the term can be related to Matthew's understanding of worship.

8. *Sebō* is used only once, in 15:9, a verse that quotes Isa 29:13 and parallels Mark 7:7. It is translated as "worship" in all versions checked except NJB, which has "reverence."

GENERAL OVERVIEW

Matthew records thirteen instances in which worship takes place:

- The Magi worship (*proskyneō*) Jesus, believing he has been born king of the Jews (2:11; see 2:2).
- A leper worships (*proskyneō*) Jesus, desiring to be cleansed (8:2).
- Crowds glorify (*doxazō*) God after Jesus heals a paralytic (9:8).
- A ruler worships (*proskyneō*) Jesus, wanting him to restore his daughter to life (9:18).

- Jesus gives thanks (*exomologeomai*) to the Father for revealing to infants what is hidden from the wise and intelligent (11:25).
- Disciples worship (*proskyneō*) Jesus, confessing him to be the Son of God (14:33).
- A Canaanite woman worships (*proskyneō*) Jesus, hoping he will heal her demon-possessed daughter (15:25).
- A crowd glorifies (*doxazō*) the God of Israel, after Jesus heals many people (15:31).
- In a parable told by Jesus, a slave worships (*proskyneō*) his king and asks for patience in payment of debts (18:26).
- The mother of James and John worships (*proskyneō*) Jesus and requests special positions for her sons (20:20).
- Children offer Jesus praise (*ainos*) in the temple, proclaiming him to be the Son of David (21:16).
- Two women worship (*proskyneō*) the risen Jesus (28:9).
- The disciples worship (*proskyneō*) the risen Jesus (28:17).

Matthew records two instances where worship does not take place:

- Herod claims he will worship (*proskyneō*) Jesus but never does (2:8).
- Satan challenges Jesus to worship (*proskyneō*) him, but Jesus does not (4:9).

Matthew records three instances of Jesus teaching or saying something about worship:

- Jesus rejects Satan by quoting the scripture that says, "Worship (*proskyneō*) the Lord your God, and serve (*latreuō*) God only" (4:10).
- Jesus tells his disciples, "Let your light shine before others, so that they may see your good works and give glory (*doxazō*) to your Father in heaven" (5:16).
- Jesus applies to the religious leaders the scripture that says, "This people honors me with their lips, but their hearts are far from me; in vain do they worship (*sebō*) me, teaching human precepts as doctrines" (15:8-9).

These texts provide the foundation for arriving at a general understanding of worship in Matthew. In addition, however, we should keep in mind the numerous references to specific *worship-related activities*. These include *(a)* prayer (5:44; 6:5-13; 7:7-11; 9:38; 14:23; 17:21var; 18:19; 19:13; 21:13, 22; 23:14var; 24:20; 26:36-44; *(b)* fasting (4:2; 6:16-18; 9:14-17; 17:21var); *(c)* blessings (14:19; 26:26) and thanksgivings (15:36; 26:27) at meals; *(d)* giving of tithes (23:23), alms (6:2-4), and other offerings (5:23; 8:4; 23:18-19); *(e)* vows (5:33-37; 23:16-22); *(f)* celebration of feasts (26:17-19) and observance of Sabbaths (12:1-12; 24:20; 28:1); and *(g)* singing (26:30).

TYPES OF WORSHIP IN MATTHEW

The thirteen instances of worship noted above are not qualitatively uniform. Three distinct types of worship are discernible.

1. Supplicatory Worship. Four times in this narrative, individuals come to Jesus, worship him, and then present him with a need or request that they hope he will address. A leper comes to Jesus, worships him, and says, "Lord, if you choose, you can make me clean" (8:2). A ruler comes to Jesus, worships him, and says, "My daughter has just died; but come and lay your hand on her, and she will live" (9:18). A Canaanite woman comes to Jesus, worships him, and says, "Lord, help me" (15:25). The mother of James and John comes to Jesus, worships him, and asks "a favor of him" (20:20). The clear pattern is *(a)* come, *(b)* worship, *(c)* present need or request.

This type of worship may be defined as *a demonstration of dependence upon and confidence in the one who is worshiped.* The two elements of dependence and confidence are present in every case.

The element of dependence is seen, first, in the seeking process through which the worshiper comes to the one who can meet the person's need. Initiative lies with the supplicant. In no instance does Jesus seek out the person in need. Dependence is further expressed through the attitude of the worshiper, who offers no rationale as to why the request should be granted. In contrast to certain psalmists, these worshipers do not point to their own merits to indicate that they deserve divine help (see, for example, Psalms 17, 26). They do not promise to respond to the granting of their boon with praise, gratitude, service, or anything else that the divine powers might desire (Pss 51:13-17; 54:6-7). In fact, Matthew is so far removed from this way of thinking that there is not a single instance in this narrative where a supplicant does express gratitude for the granting of a request (compare Luke 17:11-18). In Matthew's narrative, supplicants worship Jesus before he meets their needs, not after. When supplicants worship Jesus in Matthew's Gospel, they are acknowledging that they have no right to expect him to grant what they are about to ask and that, should he choose to grant it, they will recognize it as a favor that they can never repay. This attitude underlies all four of the worship events involving supplicants and Jesus in Matthew but is expressed most clearly in the story of the Canaanite woman. At Jesus' prompting, she compares herself to a dog that has no claim on the children's bread but hopes, nevertheless, to receive crumbs that fall from the table. In short, she refuses to provide Jesus with any rationale as to why he should help her, acknowledging instead that she merely hopes she will be so fortunate as to discover that he will. Either way, he is deserving of her worship, and he receives it before the request is granted.

Supplicatory worship in Matthew's narrative also demonstrates the confidence that the supplicant has in Jesus. This confidence is not assurance that the request will be granted but assurance that Jesus has the power or means to grant it. The attitude is expressed perfectly in the words of the leper: "If you choose, you can" (8:2). Likewise, the ruler flatly states what he knows to be true: "Lay your hand on her, and she will live" (9:18). The Canaanite woman too is absolutely certain that Jesus can heal her daughter if he is so disposed. In her case, the attitude of worship that combines awareness of dependence on Jesus with confidence in his power is described as "great faith" (15:28), in deliberate contrast to the "little faith" evidenced by Jesus' own disciples at various points (6:30; 8:26; 14:31; 16:8; 17:20).

The story that deals with the mother of James and John is unusual in that, here, a worshiping supplicant presents a request that is not granted. As in the other stories, she comes to Jesus, worships him, and then makes her plea. Her words, "Declare that these two sons of mine will sit, one at your right hand and one at your left" indicate that she believes Jesus can grant what she desires simply by commanding it and making it so. She offers no rationale as to why he should grant her request, demonstrating instead that she is confident of his power to grant it and dependent only on his willingness to do so. This is the proper attitude for a worshiping supplicant in Matthew. Jesus denies her request not because he (or God) is unable to grant it but because what she asks contravenes the will of God. The ones who are to fill the positions she wishes for her sons have already been chosen (20:23). The proper attitude of worship, then, does not guarantee a supplicant success.

The instance that involves the slave who worships his king in a parable told by Jesus is also an example of supplicatory worship, although the quality of the slave's worship does not match that of the supplicants who worship Jesus in the Gospel narrative. First, the slave does not come to the king but is brought to him (18:24). The encounter is initiated by the lord, not by the supplicant. Second, the slave does not worship the king until after his case has already been decided, in a manner that he finds unacceptable (18:25). Finally, when the slave does worship his king, he offers a rationale for why the king should grant his request: "Have patience with me, and I will pay you everything" (18:26). In short, he exhibits neither dependence on nor confidence in his lord. Despite this poor attitude of worship, the king does grant the supplicant's request, ignoring the inappropriate rationale suggested by the slave. Out of pity, the king simply forgives the slave's debt (18:26).

We may conclude, then, that a proper attitude of worship is no more a prerequisite for success in supplication than it is a guarantee for such success. Supplicatory worship in Matthew has an integrity of its own, unrelated to the granting or denial of requests. The notion that promised blessings may be an inducement to worship is Satanic (4:9). The true benefits of supplicatory worship derive not from a potential for persuasion but from a potential to solidify the relationship between the supplicant and the one whom the supplicant worships. As it turns out, the mother of James and John, who worships rightly but has her request denied, fares better than the slave, who worships poorly and has his request granted. She is still present with Jesus' followers at the end of the story (27:55-56); he incurs his lord's anger and is delivered to jailers (18:34).

That Matthew's concept of supplicatory worship is distinctive can be seen from the fact that all five passages exemplary of this kind of worship (8:2; 9:18; 15:25; 18:26; 20:20) are unique to Matthew's Gospel. In fact, neither Mark nor Luke contains any references to worship by supplicants at all. The closest either of these Gospels gets to such a reference is the one verse in Mark where the Gerasene demoniac is said to worship (*proskyneō*) Jesus (Mark 5:6). What follows this worship, however, is not a request but a command. The demoniac shouts at the top of his voice, "I adjure you by God, do not torment me" (Mark 5:7).

Now that we have defined the essential character of supplicatory worship in Matthew and observed positive and negative examples of it, we may make some observations regarding the more general theme of supplication in Matthew.

First, we may note the occasions that involve supplicants where worship is not explicitly mentioned: *(a)* a centurion comes to Jesus and says, "Lord, my servant is lying at home paralyzed" (8:5); *(b)* a disciple asks Jesus to let him go and bury his father before following him (8:21); *(c)* disciples in a storm-tossed boat say to Jesus, "Lord, save us! We are perishing!" (8:25); *(d)* demons beg Jesus, "If you cast us out, send us into the herd of swine" (8:31); *(e)* two blind men follow Jesus, crying aloud, "Have mercy on us, Son of David!" (9:27); *(f)* a man kneels before Jesus and says, "Lord, have mercy on my son, for he is an epileptic" (17:14-15); *(g)* two blind men sitting by the roadside cry out, "Have mercy on us, Son of David!" (20:30); and *(h)* Jesus prays in the garden of Gethsemane, "My Father, if it is possible, let this cup pass from me" (26:39).

All of the supplicants in these passages exhibit an attitude of total dependence on the one from whom they seek a favor. The centurion states outright that he is unworthy (8:8), and several of the others acknowledge that what they seek is "mercy," that is, an undeserved benefit (9:27; 17:15; 20:30). Even the demons recognize that Jesus is the Son of God who, if he chooses, may torment them before the time (8:29). In no case do any of these supplicants suggest a rationale for the granting of their request.

In several cases these supplicants also exhibit the attitude of confidence that we have associated with supplicatory worship. The centurion knows that his servant will be healed if Jesus but says the word (8:8). The blind men are asked by Jesus, "Do you believe I am able to do this?" and they respond, "Yes, Lord" (9:28). Jesus' own supplication includes the qualification "if it is possible" (26:39), but this is no reflection on his confidence in the power of God. Jesus knows that "for God all things are possible" (19:26) but that, paradoxically, not everything that God can do accords with God's will (see 26:53-54). In another instance, however, confidence is noticeably absent. Jesus' disciples are more fearful than confident (8:26), and they seem surprised when Jesus is able to save them as they asked (8:27).

From these accounts, we may note that an attitude of worship often accompanies supplication in Matthew's Gospel even when the act of worship is not reported. Yet these accounts also confirm what we noted earlier: the presence of this attitude serves as neither a prerequisite for the granting of the supplicant's request nor as a guarantee that it will be granted. The requests of Jesus (26:39) and of the disciple who wishes to bury his father (8:21) are not granted, even though they are brought by persons who exhibit the ideal combination of dependence and confidence. The request of the disciples in the boat (8:25) is granted, even though it is brought by persons who exhibit cowardice and "little faith." The God of Matthew's Gospel gives to good and bad alike (5:45).

We may now consider the teaching of Jesus regarding supplication in Matthew's Gospel. First, there are a number of what appear to be "blanket promises" by which Jesus encourages supplication and assures its success: (a) "Ask, and it will be given you; . . . for everyone who asks receives. . . . If you then, who are evil, know how to give good gifts to your children, how much more will your Father in heaven give good things to those who ask him!" (7:7-11); (b) "If two of you agree on earth about anything you ask, it will be done for you by my Father in heaven" (18:19); and (c) "Whatever you ask for in prayer with faith, you will receive" (21:22).

The gist of these statements may be compared with what we have already observed in the narrative of Matthew's Gospel, namely, that those who ask sometimes do not receive, even when the request is made appropriately (8:21; 20:20; 26:39). We are told that two such requests—those of the mother of James and John (20:20) and of Jesus in the garden (26:39)—are not granted, because they are out of line with the predetermined plan or will of God. Although the teaching of Jesus in this Gospel does not explicitly qualify promises of answered prayer with regard to God's will (see 1 John 5:14), the narrative context in which this teaching is set makes such a qualification implicit. Indeed, the qualification that Jesus does make, "with faith" (21:22), assumes this. In Matthew, supplicants have faith not when they presume to know the will of the one they worship but when they make their request in confidence that this one is worthy of worship regardless of whether the favor is granted (15:28). The emphasis on agreement in 18:19 also assumes that supplicants will realize that not everything they ask accords with God's will and that, for this reason, they will seek confirmation in their discernment of God's will from others in the church.

What are the good things the heavenly Father gives to those who ask? Jesus tells his disciples specifically to pray for those who persecute them (5:44), for God's name to be hallowed (6:9), for God's kingdom to come and God's will to be done (6:10), for daily bread (6:11), for forgiveness of debts (6:12), to be delivered from evil rather than led into temptation (6:13), for laborers to be sent into the harvest (9:38), for the time of flight not to be in winter or on a Sabbath (24:20), and not to enter into temptation (26:41). But over against all these encouragements is the assertion that the "Father knows what you need before you ask" (6:8; see also 6:32). Thus, there is no reason to pile up empty phrases as those do who "think that they will be heard because of their many words" (6:7). Such empty phrases, we may aver, would include rationales and other words intended to persuade the Deity. In striking contrast to Luke's Gospel (11:5-8; 18:1-8), supplication is never presented as a strategy of persuasion in Matthew. Here, the model prayer that Jesus teaches (6:7-13) is above all a model of simple and direct expression. Supplicants are expected to acknowledge their dependence on and confidence in the Deity and then they are simply to state what they desire.

2. Responsive Worship. A second type of worship in Matthew's Gospel is that which is offered as grateful response. Three times in this narrative, individuals or groups praise God in response to something that has happened. Matthew concludes the story of Jesus healing a paralytic by saying, "When the crowds saw it, they were filled with awe, and they glorified God, who had given such authority to human beings" (9:8). Another time he records that Jesus healed many people, "so that the crowd was amazed when they saw the mute speaking, the maimed whole, the lame walking, and the blind seeing. And they praised (*doxazō*) the God of Israel" (15:31). And on another occasion Jesus himself declares, "I thank you, Father, Lord of heaven and earth, because you have hidden these things from the wise and the intelligent and have revealed them to infants" (11:25). This type of worship may be defined as *a response that acknowledges and celebrates activity attributed to the one who is worshiped.* Again, it is the combination of two elements, acknowledgment and celebration, that characterizes this type of worship in Matthew.

In all three of the cases cited, the worshipers acknowledge that God is responsible for something that might have been attributed to another. When Jesus heals the paralytic, demonstrating that "the Son of Man has authority on earth" (9:6), the crowd does not glorify him for possessing such authority. Rather, they glorify God for giving such authority to humans. Again, in Matthew 15, they glorify the God of Israel for the many healings that are being performed ostensibly by Jesus. Jesus' prayer of thanksgiving to the Father also incorporates this element of acknowledgment. Although the context for the prayer is somewhat ambiguous, Jesus evidently observes that those whom he calls "infants" know some things that those whom he calls "the wise and the intelligent" do not know. His response to this observation is not to praise the infants for their superior perception but to give thanks to God for revealing things to infants and hiding things from others. In short, his thanksgiving acknowledges that God is responsible for the current state of affairs.

Responsive worship in Matthew also includes an element of celebration. Jesus' prayer to the Father attributes the hiding and revealing of things to God's *gracious will* (*eudokia*). What God has done is good. In the two episodes involving the crowds, the element of celebration is inherent in the word *doxazō* ("glorify"). The crowds do not simply recognize that God has given extraordinary authority to humans; they glorify the God who has done this, indicating that what God has done is good.

We may consider whether supplicatory worship and responsive worship are related to each other. Does not the one precede divine activity and the other follow it? Such a connection may seem logical to us, but in Matthew's Gospel the two forms of worship never occur together. The stories in which supplicants worship Jesus and make their needs known to him are completely different episodes from those in which people take note of something God has done and respond with worship. In fact, as we noted earlier, supplicants themselves are never portrayed as offering thanksgiving in Matthew's Gospel. The paralytic whom Jesus heals, the mute who speak, the maimed who are made whole, the lame who walk, the blind who see, the infants who receive divine revelation—these are not the ones who glorify God and give thanks. In every instance of responsive worship reported in this narrative, the worshipers are not the persons who have benefited from the divine activity but are persons who acknowledge and celebrate what God has done *for others*. This is not at all the case in the Gospel of Luke, which frequently describes people who worship God in response to what God has done for them (5:25; 13:13; 17:15-16; 18:43) and once records a rebuke by Jesus of people who do not (17:17-18). There is nothing in Matthew that suggests that supplicants or others would be wrong to offer thanksgiving for what God has done for them, but thanksgiving for one's own blessings is clearly not a point to be emphasized in this book. Instead, it presents supplicants as persons who worship even before their requests have been granted, and it presents responsive worshipers as persons who glorify God for good fortune bestowed on others.

We may now consider the relationship that Matthew's presentation of responsive worship bears to an overall theme of "response" in this Gospel. Amid the diversity of responses that people show to the works of God wrought by Jesus,[7] three stand out as particularly common:[8]

   a. Hostility or rejection—people accuse Jesus of collusion with the devil (9:34; 12:24); they are offended (*skandalizō*) by him

---

7. Responses to the words or teaching of Jesus in Matthew include accusation (9:3; 26:65), amazement (22:22; 27:14), astonishment (7:25; 19:25; 22:33), compliance (3:15; 4:11, 20, 22; 9:9; 21:6; 26:19), confusion (16:7), distress (17:23), following (8:23), perception (21:45), questioning (17:10, 19; 18:21; 19:10, 25, 27; 21:10; 24:3), resistance (16:22), ridicule (9:24), silence (22:46), and understanding (16:12; 17:13).
   8. Other responses to Jesus' works include service (8:15) and terror (14:26).

(13:57) and indignant (*aganakteō*) at him (21:15), they beg him to leave (8:34) and plot outright to destroy him (12:14). Jesus predicts that such responses will continue to be typical for the ministry his disciples are to conduct in the world (10:16-25; 24:9-14). Matthew's readers are clearly expected to regard such responses as unfortunate and inappropriate.

b. Amazement—people are astonished (*ekplēssomai*, 13:54), amazed (*thaumazō*, 8:27; 9:33; 15:31; 21:20), and astounded (*existēmi*, 12:23) by Jesus. These responses are simply neutral. Jesus himself can be amazed (*thaumazō*, 8:10) and describe the Lord's doing as "amazing (*thaumastē*) in our eyes" (21:42). Amazement can be associated with worship (15:31), but it can also be a sign of "little faith" (8:26-27) or an expression of those who are hostile to Jesus (22:22; 27:14). Astonishment is even characterized as "unbelief" in one passage (13:54, 58).

c. Acclaim—people respond to Jesus by spreading his fame abroad (4:24; 9:26, 31); following him in great crowds (4:25; 8:1; 14:13; 20:39; compare 20:34) and bringing to him their sick in expectation that he will continue to heal (4:24; 9:2; 14:35; 15:30). At first glance, such responses may seem positive, but we should note that Jesus never seeks such acclaim in Matthew and, at times, appears to resist it by withdrawing from the crowds (14:33; 15:21). Once, the response of acclaim is depicted as the opposite of what Jesus wants (9:31), brought about through disobedience to his command, "See that no one knows of this" (9:30).

We may conclude, then, that the infrequent response of worship is preferable in Matthew to the more common responses of hostility, amazement, and acclaim. When the crowds glorify God for what Jesus has done (9:33; 15:31), they respond in a manner that is neither negative nor ambiguous but in keeping with what Jesus himself has described as the appropriate response to good works by God's agents (5:16).

Still, if worship is an appropriate response, it is not the ideal one. For Matthew, the ideal response to divine activity is repentance.[9] Jesus begins his ministry by announcing, "Repent, for the

9. The parable of the Sower presents the ideal response to the word of the kingdom as "the bearing of fruit" by those who hear the word and understand

kingdom of heaven has come near (4:17; see 3:2; 10:7). The
crowds who witness Jesus' healings and exorcisms ought to realize that the kingdom of God has come to them (12:28) and they
ought, accordingly, to repent. Indeed, Jesus never upbraids
people for failing to worship or give thanks in this Gospel (compare Luke 17:17-18), but he does upbraid those who have wit-
nessed his mighty works and not repented (11:20-24). We know
from Jesus' teaching in Matthew that people can worship God
with their lips even when their deeds demonstrate that their
hearts are far from God (7:3-9). Thus, the responsive worship of
the crowds in 9:8 and 15:31 is commendable but will be in vain if
performed with unrepentant hearts.

3. Epiphanic Worship. A third type of worship in Matthew is
that which is associated with some manifestation of divine presence. Five times in Matthew's Gospel groups of people worship
Jesus in simple recognition of who he is. The Magi come and
worship Jesus because they have been led to believe that he is
"king of the Jews" (2:2, 11). Jesus' disciples worship him in a boat
when his manifestation to them there convinces them that he is
the Son of God (14:33). Children in the temple praise Jesus by
shouting, "Hosanna to the Son of David" (21:15). Two women
worship Jesus when he appears to them risen from the dead
(28:9), and, finally, his disciples do the same when he also appears
to them on the mountain in Galilee (28:17). In all of these cases,
the focus of worship is not anticipation of what Jesus might do or
response to what Jesus has done. The focus is on Jesus himself,
on who he is revealed to be.

Epiphanic worship may be defined as *a participation in divine
revelation that clarifies and expresses the worshiper's perception of the
one who is worshiped.* All five of the cases involve an element of
divine revelation, and in all five cases the worshipers' perception
of Jesus is clarified and expressed.

In the story of the Magi, the element of divine revelation is
evident in the star that draws these persons first from the East
(2:2) and finally to the very house where the child lives (2:9). Par-

---

it (13:8, 23). The fruit that is thus borne surely includes "fruit worthy of repentance" (3:8).

ticipation in this event leads them to recognize Jesus as the one who is born king of the Jews (2:2). For Jesus' disciples, the epiphany occurs when Jesus comes to them at night, walking on the sea, when he allows Peter to attempt the same, and when the wind ceases as he and Peter get back into the boat. These remarkable occurrences prompt the disciples to confess Jesus as the Son of God, a confession that Jesus claims can be made by humans only when it is revealed to them by the Father (16:17). The element of divine revelation is also evident in the story of the children in the temple. Jesus quotes scripture to indicate that the children's praise has been "prepared" or "brought forth" (*katartizō*) by God (21:16). In addition, Jesus' reference to "infants" (*nēpioi*) serves to identify the worshipers here with those to whom he says the Father reveals things that are hidden from the wise and the intelligent (11:25).

The final two instances of epiphanic worship occur in the context of the resurrection, the ultimate manifestation of divine presence in Matthew. The women first encounter an angel who reveals that Jesus is alive and commissions them to take a message to his disciples. Then, they encounter the risen Lord himself, who confirms what the angel has said (28:10). Their worship of Jesus derives from their participation in this divine manifestation and expresses their recognition of Jesus as a risen Lord who ordains them for mission. Likewise, when the disciples see Jesus on the mountain, their worship expresses their acceptance of him as one who has indeed risen from the dead, as one who possesses all authority in heaven and on earth, and as one who will be with them always to the close of the age (28:17-20).

One other instance that might be considered under the heading of epiphanic worship in Matthew is the account of the transfiguration in 17:1-8. Matthew does not explicitly say that the disciples worship Jesus when he is transfigured before them, but they do prostrate themselves (like the Magi in 2:11 and the women in 28:9) and are filled with fear (compare 28:8). Matthew also does not tell us how the disciples' perception of Jesus is clarified or expressed through their participation in this event, but he indicates that something must have been revealed to them when Jesus commands them not to tell anyone "the vision" until after the Son of Man has been raised from the dead (17:9).

We may now consider how Matthew's description of epiphanic worship accords with this Gospel's treatment of epiphanies and revelation in general. In Matthew's story, divine revelation comes not only through scripture, which is the word of God (15:6), but also through angels (1:20; 2:13, 19; 28:2, 5-7), prophets (11:9; 23:4), dreams (1:20; 2:13, 19), and the occurrence of remarkable events (27:51-54). Jesus' words, furthermore, indicate that manifestations of divine presence will continue beyond the temporal setting of Matthew's story into the time of Matthew's readers. Jesus will be with his disciples until "the end of the age" (28:20). Whenever two or three gather in his name, he will be among them (18:20). Specifically, he will be present in missionaries (10:40), in children (18:5), and in members of his "family" who experience various needs (25:35-36). But not all these manifestations are occasions for worship or even for revelation. Sometimes Jesus' presence will not be recognized (25:37-40, 44-45).

At least one worship event, however, is connected directly to the epiphanic manifestation of Christ's presence and the potential for revelation that this entails. By identifying the bread and wine of the Passover meal with his own body and blood (26:26-28), Jesus provides that meal with a new epiphanic and eschatological interpretation. Matthew's readers are to celebrate the Passover not "in remembrance" of Jesus (Luke 22:19; 1 Cor 11:24-25) but in recognition of his continuing presence among them (18:20; 28:20) and in anticipation of the day when they will drink wine anew with Jesus in the Father's kingdom (26:29). If such a celebration is consistent with Matthew's presentation of epiphanic worship elsewhere, it will involve a participation in divine revelation that both clarifies and expresses the worshipers' perception of Jesus. In this case, Matthew indicates, such revelation will focus on the worshipers' relationship to Jesus as one who initiates a new covenant and forgives sins (26:28) and as one who, like them, awaits the consummation of God's reign (26:29) inaugurated through his own words (4:17) and deeds (12:28).[10]

10. Studies on Matthew's view of the eucharist are few, perhaps because, while scholars debate whether the Markan, Lukan, or Pauline account of the supper is most original (see Bradshaw, 47), no one accords this status to the Matthean version. On the eucharist in the New Testament (with some reference

FORMS OF WORSHIP

The details that Matthew provides concerning the actual forms that worship takes are sparse but they do enable us to identify three things that acts of worship may include:

a. A shift in physical posture.[11]   The word *proskyneō* is a combination of *pros* ("toward") and *kyneō* ("to kiss") and thus seems to carry a root meaning of bowing, bending, or in some other sense altering one's physical posture with regard to the object of worship. In practical usage, however, the word can refer to the inner attitude of obeisance or homage regardless of whether this is demonstrated through overt physical action. Matthew uses the term thirteen times but supplements it with additional phraseology when the physical action is emphasized. Twice in Matthew worshipers are described as "falling down" (*piptō*) before the one whom they worship (2:11; 18:26), and once a group of worshipers is said to "take hold of Jesus' feet," which must imply a similar prostration (28:9). Others are also described as "falling down" in passages where worship is not explicitly mentioned (17:6; 18:29), and Jesus falls "on his face" when he prays in the garden (26:39). In 17:14 a supplicant is described as kneeling (*gonypeteō*). Soldiers also kneel before Jesus in a mockery of worship in 27:29. Notably, when Satan seeks to be worshiped, he specifically requests that Jesus "fall down (*piptō*) and worship (*proskyneō*)" him (4:9).

---

to Matthew), see Bradshaw, 131–60; Delling, 135–50; A. J. B. Higgins, *The Lord's Supper in the New Testament* (SBT 6; Chicago: Henry Regnery Co., 1952); Joachim Jeremias, *The Eucharistic Words of Jesus*, trans. Norman Perrin (London: SCM Press, 1966); Jerome Kodell, *The Eucharist in the New Testament* (Wilmington, Del.: Michael Glazier, 1988); Xavier Léon-Dufour, *Sharing the Eucharistic Bread: The Witness of the New Testament* (New York: Paulist Press, 1982); I. Howard Marshall, *Last Supper and Lord's Supper* (Grand Rapids: Wm. B. Eerdmans, 1980); Martin, 110–29; Moule, 18–46; John Reumann, *The Supper of the Lord: The New Testament, Ecumenical Dialogues, and Faith and Order on Eucharist* (Philadelphia: Fortress Press, 1985), 1–52; Eduard Schweizer, *The Lord's Supper according to the New Testament*, trans. James M. Davis (Philadelphia: Fortress Press, 1967); and Dennis E. Smith and Hal E. Taussing, *Many Tables: The Eucharist in the New Testament and Liturgy Today* (London: SCM Press, 1990).

11. On this form of worship, see M. I. Gruber, *Aspects of Nonverbal Communication in the Ancient Near East* (StP 12/1; Rome: Biblical Institute, 1980), 90–151.

In three passages where Synoptic parallels describe shifts in physical posture Matthew has no indication of the manner in which worship takes place. Mark 1:40 describes the leper as kneeling before Jesus, and Luke 5:12 says he falls on his face. Mark 5:22 and Luke 8:41 both describe the ruler who comes to Jesus as falling at his feet. Mark 7:25 indicates that the Syro-Phoenician woman also falls at Jesus' feet. In all three of these stories, Matthew says the person worships (*proskyneō*) Jesus, while the Synoptic parallels do not, yet the Synoptic parallels describe a shift in physical posture not mentioned in Matthew (8:2; 9:18; 15:25). In these stories of supplicatory worship, at least, Matthew presents worship as an attitude of a person toward Jesus while ignoring the manner in which this attitude is displayed.

b. Verbal expression.   What is described as worship in Matthew takes the form of a verbal prayer of thanksgiving once (11:25-26) and the form of confessional acclamation twice (14:33; 21:15). Elsewhere in the Gospel, Jesus' blessings (14:19; 26:26) and thanksgivings (15:36; 26:27) at meals probably take the form of verbal expression, although this is not specified. To these we might add the sole reference to singing in 26:30.

Worship through verbal expression is critiqued by Jesus' citation of scripture to indicate that hypocrites may worship God with their lips while their hearts are far from God (15:8). The implication is that worship through verbal expression is "in vain" unless this worship is from the heart.

c. Offering of gifts.   The giving of gifts is explicitly associated with worship only once in Matthew, in the story of the Magi and the infant Jesus (2:11). This story forms an ironic contrast to that of Satan in 4:9-10. Whereas Jesus receives gifts from worshipers, Satan must offer gifts to (potential) worshipers and even then is unable to secure their devotion.

If orientation of the heart is what counts in worship (15:8), we might expect that offerings of gifts would be an especially appropriate form of worship, since Jesus says, "Where your treasure (*thesauros*) is, there your heart will be also" (6:21). When the Magi give of their treasure (*thesauros*) to Jesus they demonstrate a devotion to him that goes beyond lip service. Still, this form of worship is critiqued by Jesus also, in four separate passages: (1) A person who needs to be reconciled with another should not bring a gift to the altar until that reconciliation has taken place (5:23-24); (2) hypocrites may pervert the meaning of offerings by giving alms so that they themselves might be glorified (6:2); (3) persons who suggest that money which might have been spent caring for elderly parents should be given to God nullify God's commandments (15:3-6); and (4) tithers sometimes neglect the weightier matters of the law: justice and mercy and faith (23:23).

The common theme in these four critiques of gift giving is a concern for relationships with other human beings. While the giving of gifts supposedly represents an orientation of the heart toward God (6:21), the gesture means little if the worshiper's relationships with other human beings are characterized by a failure to achieve reconciliation, a desire for glory, or a neglect of the basic concerns for support and compassion that are central to the will of God for humanity. In other words, the love for God that worship is expected to convey needs to be connected with love for neighbor (22:37-40). Another, possibly implicit critique of gift giving would be compatible with this perspective, although we must construct it from silence. Matthew's Gospel contains no accounts or references to offerings of gifts presented by the poor. This may be because, in recognition of a higher concern for justice and mercy, the poor should not be expected to worship in this way. We cannot be sure, but we may note that in this Gospel widows are not commended for giving their last pennies to religious institutions (compare Mark 12:41-44; Luke 21:1-4).[12]

This primary concern for the attitude or orientation of the worshiper applies to other forms of worship besides gift giving. Jesus' critique of verbal expression in 15:7-9 is directly connected to his criticism of gift giving in 15:3-6. Giving to God what should have been used for elderly parents is an indication that hearts are far from God and, thus, that worship with the lips is in vain. Likewise, what Jesus says about giving alms in order to be glorified by people applies to all forms of piety (6:1), including prayer (6:5-6) and fasting (6:16-18). Hence we see that the few comments Jesus does have to make concerning forms of worship

---

12. Some scholars even question whether Jesus' words concerning the widow in Mark and Luke should be read as commendations. See Elizabeth Struthers Malbon, "The Poor Widow in Mark and Her Poor Rich Readers," *CBQ* 53 (1991): 539–604.

in Matthew derive from an overriding concern with attitude: almsgivers should not blow trumpets (6:2); people should pray in private rooms rather than in synagogues or at street corners (6:5-6); fasters should anoint their heads and wash their faces (6:17). Why? Not because there is an intrinsically right way to perform these actions but because piety should be practiced with an attitude that seeks no glory from others (6:1).

Conclusion. What is perhaps most notable with regard to forms of worship in Matthew is that in seven of the thirteen instances in which acts of worship are explicitly reported nothing whatsoever is said about the manner in which this worship takes place (8:2; 9:8, 18; 15:25, 31; 20:20; 28:17). When the crowds glorify God in 9:8 and 15:31, what precisely do they do? Do they say prayers of thanksgiving similar to that attributed to Jesus in 11:25-26? Do they fall down? Do they sing hymns? Do they dance in the streets? Matthew simply does not say. In sum, Matthew's Gospel is sketchy with regard to forms of worship, and what is revealed is presented as less significant than the attitude with which the worship is carried out. The desired attitude is the orientation toward God and neighbor described elsewhere in the narrative as "love" (*agapē*).

MOODS OF WORSHIP

Matthew's Gospel is also quite restrained in its description of moods (emotional or psychological dispositions) of worshipers. Still, we may identify four moods that accompany worship at least once in this narrative:

1. Joy. The Magi are "overwhelmed with joy" (*echarēsan charan mēgalēn sphodra*) just prior to their worship of Jesus (2:10) and the women depart the empty tomb with "great joy" (*charas mēgalēs*) just before they meet the risen Lord and worship him (28:8). The first passage is notable for its redundant superlatives, while the latter stands out for the contrast it presents to the picture in Mark 16:8 where the women's flight from the tomb is characterized by "trembling" (*tromos*) and "astonishment" (*ekstasis*). If Matthew seems to emphasize joy in these passages, however, Luke's Gospel is the one that records Jesus as rejoicing (*agalliaō*) in the Holy Spirit when he gives thanks to the Father (Luke 10:21). Matthew's account of this thanksgiving is more sober (Matt 11:25). Luke also connects the praise Jesus receives when he enters Jerusalem with rejoicing (*chairō*), while Matthew does not (Luke 19:37; Matt 21:9).[13] Other references to joy in Matthew indicate that it is essentially an eschatological phenomenon. The discovery of the kingdom of heaven elicits a joy that compels one to give up all that one has to attain it (13:44). Jesus' inauguration of God's reign entails a recovery of "little ones" that is also cause for rejoicing (18:13). At the end of the age God's faithful servants will be invited to enter into the joy of their master (25:21, 23). Even now, then, those who are persecuted for Christ's sake may rejoice (*chairō*) and be glad (*agalliaō*), knowing that their reward in heaven is great (5:12).

Still, joy can be superficial. In Jesus' parable of the Sower, the seed that falls on rocky soil is likened to one who hears the word and "immediately receives it with joy (*chara*)," yet "has no root, but endures only for a while, and when trouble or persecution arises on account of the word" immediately falls away (13:20-21). Thus, joy may be an appropriate mood for worship that celebrates God's kingdom, but such joy provides no evidence that the "word of the kingdom" (13:19) has taken root and will bear fruit.

2. Fear. The crowds who glorify God after Jesus heals a paralytic are described in Matthew 9:8 as "afraid" (*phobeomai*). Elsewhere, disciples are "terrified" (*tarassō*) and cry out with fear (*phobos*) shortly before they worship Jesus in a boat (14:26, 33) and women depart the empty tomb in fear (*phobos*) just before

13. If Luke's Gospel contains more references to worship and employs a broader vocabulary for worship than Matthew's, the same is true for the theme of joy. Aside from one use of *agalliaō* (5:12), Matthew uses only *chairō* (2:10; 5:12; 18:13) and *chara* (2:10; 13:20, 44; 25:21, 23; 28:8). Luke not only uses these terms more generously (*agalliaō*, 1:47; 10:21; *chairō*, 1:14; 6:23; 10:20; 13:17; 15:5, 32; 19:6, 37; 22:5; 23:8; *chara*, 1:14; 2:10; 8:13; 10:17; 15:7, 10; 24:41, 52) but also employs *agalliasis* (1:14, 44), *euphrainō* (12:19; 15:23, 24, 29, 32; 16:19), *skirtaō* (1:41, 44; 6:23), and *synchairō* (1:58; 15:6, 9). Mark's Gospel is the most sparse, using only *hēdeōs* in 6:20 and 12:37 plus *chairō* (14:11) and *chara* (4:16) once apiece in negative contexts.

they encounter the risen Jesus and worship him (28:8-9). The latter two references are paralleled in Mark's Gospel (Mark 6:50; 16:8), although Mark never connects fear with worship.

A distinction is drawn in Matthew's Gospel between fear of the world, especially human beings, and fear of God. The former is invariably restrictive[14] and, from an eschatological perspective, unnecessary (10:26, 28, 31). Worship should never be associated with this type of fear, for only hypocrites practice piety with a view to what others think of them (6:1-18). Fear of God, however, is imperative (10:28), and this is the type of fear envisioned when the worshipers mentioned in 9:8; 14:33; and 28:9 respond to manifestations of divine presence with fear.[15] In two of these cases Jesus tells the worshipers *not* to be afraid (14:33; 28:10), but this should not be taken as a rebuke or sign that the fear was inappropriate. Rather, Jesus' response brings out the dialogical potential of divine/human encounters. While worshipers may appropriately fear the one they worship, those who are worthy of worship may also seek to attenuate the fear of their worshipers.

In addition to the three passages we have cited where fear is explicitly associated with worship, Matthew depicts people responding to divine manifestations with fear in four other instances: Herod is terrified (*tarassō*) by the Magi's assertion that heavenly portents have announced the birth of a new king (2:3); Jesus' disciples are afraid (*phobeomai*) when they hear the voice of God at the transfiguration (17:6); the centurion and other soldiers at Jesus' crucifixion are filled with fear (*phobeomai*) when they see the stupendous events that accompany Jesus' death (27:54); and the guard at the tomb trembles with fear (*phobos*) in the presence of an angel who rolls away the stone (28:4). From these passages we see that fear of the divine can generate a variety of responses: Herod takes aggressive action to kill the Messiah (2:7-8, 16-18); the disciples fall on their faces in an action per-

14. Fear prevents or would prevent people from doing what they would do if they were not afraid: take a wife (1:20); settle in a particular area (2:22); kill an enemy (14:5); walk on water (14:30); speak one's mind (21:26); make an arrest (21:46); invest money (25:25).

15. Absent from Matthew's Gospel are three passages in Mark where people fear Jesus apart from any demonstration of divine power (Mark 9:32; 10:32; 11:18).

haps representative of worship (17:6); the soldiers proclaim that
Jesus was certainly the Son of God (27:54); and the guards at the
tomb become paralyzed, "like dead men" (28:4).

In Matthew's Gospel, then, there is no intrinsic connection
between the fear of God and worship. In and of itself, fear of God
is neither positive nor negative. People ought to fear God, and
usually do, because God is fearsome (10:28). Still, fearing God
and worshiping God are distinct though compatible phenomena.

3. Amazement. In one instance (15:31), worshipers are described in Matthew as "amazed" (*thaumazō*). We have already
discussed amazement as a response to Jesus in the section on responsive worship above. It is an appropriate mood for worship
because the Lord's doing truly is amazing (*thaumastē*) in human
eyes (21:42), but amazement is not in itself a mark of faith (8:26-
27) or devotion (22:22; 27:14).

4. Doubt. Worship is associated with doubt (*distazō*) twice in
Matthew's Gospel, in the only two passages where Jesus' disciples are presented as worshipers. Jesus calls attention to Peter's
doubt just before he and the other disciples worship Jesus in a
boat (14:31-33). On Easter morning eleven disciples respond to
the risen Jesus with worship and doubt (28:17). In the first of
these passages, doubt is linked to fear (of the world, not of God),
and the one who doubts is also described as a person of "little
faith" (14:30-31).

As a matter of fine tuning, we may ask whether the doubters in
these two passages are actually among the ones who worship.
Matthew 14:33 can be read as implying that those in the boat *exclusive of Peter* (who doubts) worship Jesus. The more natural interpretation, however, takes 14:32 as indicative that doubting
Peter is now among the worshipers in the boat. Otherwise, we
are left with the unlikely prospect of regarding the disciples who
did not even try to walk on water as having superior faith to Peter
who tried but failed. Likewise, Matthew 28:17 can be read as implying that some of the eleven disciples worship Jesus while
others doubt. English translations have generally favored this
reading on the assumption that worship and doubt are incompatible, but such a reading is less natural grammatically than one

that ascribes both worship and doubt to all eleven disciples.[16] In any case, Matthew's Gospel is more interested in the attitude of the community as a whole than in the particular attitudes of individuals and in this regard the evidence is clear: the presence of doubt in the community does not prevent the community from worshiping.

Although the word *distazō* does not occur elsewhere in Matthew (or in all of the New Testament), a possible synonym, *diakrinomai*, is used in Matthew 21:21 when Jesus promises success at moving mountains to those who "have faith and do not doubt." This verse would seem to indicate that doubt is a lack of faith that prevents God's people from achieving what would be possible otherwise. This harsh view is mitigated somewhat, however, by a similar saying of Jesus in Matthew 17:20 where "faith the size of a mustard seed" is held to be sufficient not only for moving mountains but for assuring that "nothing will be impossible." Thus, doubt implies a lack but not a total absence of faith, and since even the tiniest amount of faith is sufficient, doubt does not preclude worship among people of "little faith" (6:30; 8:26; 14:31; 16:8; 17:20).

Conclusion. Of the thirteen explicit acts of worship reported in Matthew's narrative, seven occasions offer no indication whatsoever for the mood of the worshiper(s) (8:2; 9:18, 18; 11:25; 15:25; 18:26; 20:20; 21:16). Of the four moods that are presented at least once, none is linked to worship through any connection that seems intrinsic or necessary. Furthermore, neither the teaching of Jesus nor the comments of the narrator offer any evaluative comments for rating one mood above another. Matthew's readers are given no reason to believe, for instance, that the joyful worship of the Magi (2:11) is superior to the amazed worship of the crowds (15:31) or the doubting worship of the dis-

16. Although *hoi de* is sometimes partitive in classical usage, all occurrences in Matthew clearly refer to the entire group of people that has previously been mentioned (2:9; 4:20, 22; 8:32; 9:31; 20:5, 31; 22:5; 27:66; 28:15) or else to persons within that group whose perspectives are to be taken as representative of the group as a whole (2:5; 14:17; 16:7, 14; 21:25; 27:21, 23). See Keith Howard Reeves, *The Resurrection Narrative in Matthew: A Literary-Critical Examination* (Lewiston, N.Y.: Edwin Mellen Press, 1993), 69–74.

ciples (14:33; 28:17). We may conclude, then, that mood is in no sense definitive of worship for Matthew. Joy, fear, amazement, and doubt are simply natural reactions that might accompany worship but that do not affect the integrity of worship one way or the other.

WORSHIPERS IN MATTHEW

Although the instances of worship described in Matthew's Gospel are relatively few, the people who are depicted as worshipers in these episodes are a diverse lot. They are inclusive with regard to age, number, sex, health, ethnic status, and economic class.

Age. Most of the worshipers are adults, but in 21:15, Matthew makes special mention of children[17] and even alludes to Psalm 8:2 to say that divinely prepared praise comes "out of the mouths of infants and nursing babies" (21:16). Since the children (*paidas*) shouting "Hosanna!" in the temple are obviously not infants or nursing babies, the effect of the scriptural reference is to extend the age range for worshipers in Matthew even further than that which is actually illustrated within the narrative. Matthew's Gospel is the only Gospel to depict children, much less infants, as worshipers. We must look to the Gospel of Luke, however, to find the age range of worshipers extended in the opposite direction, that is, to include the elderly (Luke 2:36-37)

Number. Individuals are depicted as worshipers six times in Matthew's Gospel (8:2; 9:18; 11:25; 15:25; 18:26; 20:20). Groups of people are depicted as worshipers seven times (2:11; 9:8; 14:33; 15:31; 21:9; 28:9, 17). Although all reported incidents of supplicatory worship concern individuals, Matthew's Gospel speaks of supplication by communities as well—note the plural "our" in the model prayer (6:9) and the emphasis on agreement in 18:19. Likewise, although all the reported incidents of epiphanic worship involve groups, Matthew knows of private epiphanies also (1:20-21).

---

17. Children may also be part of the crowds who glorify God in 9:8 and 15:31. Although not specifically mentioned there, they are said to be among the crowds fed by Jesus in 14:21 and 15:38.

Sex. Matthew's Gospel mentions three occasions where women are worshipers (15:25; 20:20; 28:9) and six occasions where men are worshipers (8:2; 9:18; 11:25; 14:33; 18:26; 28:17). In addition, Matthew includes four references to groups of worshipers (Magi,[18] crowds) that may include both men and women.

Health. The leper who worships Jesus in 8:2 is a diseased and "unclean" individual. The other worshipers mentioned in Matthew's Gospel are apparently healthy.[19]

Ethnic Status. The Magi who worship Jesus are Gentiles who have come "from the East" (2:1), a vague designation that emphasizes their foreignness. The Canaanite woman is a representative of the indigenous population that Israelites once apportioned for genocide and have continued to regard as pagan and unclean. The rest of the worshipers mentioned in Matthew are probably Jewish, although the ethnic status of the ruler in 9:18 and of the slave in 18:26 remains ambiguous.[20]

Economic Class. The Magi are worshipers who belong to the upper end of the economic scale. Their wealth is emphasized in Matthew's narrative when they are described as "opening their treasures" and offering expensive gifts to Jesus (2:11). Designation of the man who worships Jesus in 9:18 as "a ruler" and subsequent mention of flute players at the funeral of this man's daughter (9:23) imply that he too is a worshiper of some means. The economic status of other worshipers in Matthew is undesignated and, apparently, not an issue. We are probably expected to regard these persons (including the crowds and the disciples) as people whose socio-economic position is average or typical for

18. Contrary to popular notions, the Magi are not "wise men" or "kings" but persons who practice astrology or other forms of oriental magic (see Gen 41:8; Esth 1:13; Dan 2:12; Acts 8:9). Such persons might be male or female.

19. Jesus' disciples (who worship him in 14:33 and 28:17) include persons who are described in a nonliteral sense as sick and in need of a physician (9:9-12).

20. Matthew's readers are not expected to regard the man in 9:18 as a *synagogue* ruler (cf. Mark 5:22; Luke 8:41), for in Matthew's story the religious leaders of Israel are unanimously opposed to Jesus and would never worship him.

most of the population. Matthew's Gospel lacks any explicit mention of worshipers who come from the lower end of the economic scale, except for the slave in 18:26 whose example proves negative. Luke's Gospel, which mentions a beggar who glorifies God in 18:43 (compare Matt 9:27-31; 20:29-34), also presents the baby Jesus as inspiring worship among peasant shepherds (Luke 2:20), a stark contrast to the wealthy Magi in Matthew 2:11.

SETTINGS FOR WORSHIP IN MATTHEW

Worship takes place in a variety of settings in Matthew: once in a house (2:11), once in a boat (14:33), once in the temple (21:16), and twice on the mountain in Galilee (15:29-31; 28:16-17). Specific settings are not indicated for the other eight instances of worship reported, although in at least five of these cases the location appears to be out-of-doors (8:2; 9:8; 11:25; 15:25; 28:9).[21]

The most noteworthy observation we can make concerning Matthew's worship settings is that worship never occurs in synagogues in this Gospel (compare Luke 4:15; 13:13). Synagogues are places where hypocrites hope they will be glorified (6:2), but they are not places where anyone ever glorifies God. Likewise, the temple is a setting for worship only once in Matthew (compare Luke 1:64; 2:28, 37; 24:53), and on that occasion the chief priests and the scribes who are in charge of the temple disapprove of the worship that transpires there (21:15).

This dearth of references to religious institutions serving as settings for worship may have a theological basis that goes beyond first-century Jewish/Christian rivalry. The notion that any particular locale serves as a quintessential setting for worship is critiqued by Jesus' claim that he will be present *wherever* two or three gather in his name (18:20). Matthew is willing to grant that God does (or did) dwell in the Jewish temple (23:21), but Matthew also insists that in Jesus "something greater than the temple" has come (12:6). In other words, the manifestation of

---

21. In two cases, the setting is out-of-doors in Matthew, where it is indoors in the Markan parallel (9:1-8, par Mark 2:1-12; 15:21-28, par Mark 7:24-30). But in one instance, the reverse is true (9:18, par Mark 5:21-23).

God's presence in Jesus Christ relativizes the significance of all
other loci where God has previously been sought or found. God
is now "with us" through Jesus (1:23) who, in turn, is encountered in missionaries (10:40), children (18:5), and the "least of his
family" (25:40). By emphasizing the continuing presence of God
among people (28:20), Matthew invites us to consider the question of "setting" along different lines. Geographical or architec-
tural locale is irrelevant, but the presence of persons through
whom Christ may be encountered is not. Private rooms may be
appropriate for individual prayer (6:6), but according to Matthew
the ideal setting for worship is a community of people gathered
in Jesus' name, wherever that may be.

RECIPIENTS OF WORSHIP
IN MATTHEW

Matthew's Gospel also reveals some diversity with regard to recipients of worship. In the thirteen instances of worship noted,
God is worshiped three times (9:8; 11:25; 15:31), Jesus is worshiped nine times (2:11; 8:2; 9:18; 14:33; 15:25; 20:20; 21:16;
28:9, 17), and a human king who is a character in a parable told
by Jesus is worshiped once (18:26). This diversity of recipients,
furthermore, corresponds somewhat to the types of worship discernible in Matthew. Responsive worship is offered only to God
in Matthew and is, in fact, the only type of worship offered to
God in Matthew. Epiphanic worship and supplicatory worship
(with the exception of 18:26) are offered only to Jesus.

With regard to responsive worship, we note that Matthew
avoids attributing praise to Jesus even in instances where this
would be natural. When *Jesus* heals people, the crowds glorify
God in response (9:8; 15:31). Since we know from references to
other types of worship that Matthew has no aversion to attributing worship to Jesus, we must ask why in these particular instances the glory is given to God. Matthew most likely wants to
depict Jesus' ministry as illustrative of a principle he has expounded elsewhere in the Gospel. Jesus tells his disciples in 5:16,
"Let your light shine before others, so that they may see your
good works and give glory to your Father in heaven." Conversely, he denounces hypocrites in 6:2 as people who do what
are ostensibly good works "so that they may be praised by

others." Matthew thinks that God's people ought to live in a way that brings glory to God rather than to themselves. Even though Jesus is one deserving of worship, he is depicted in Matthew's narrative as one whose good works bring glory to God rather than to himself. This point, incidentally, is unique to Matthew's Gospel. Neither Mark nor Luke has any parallel to the sayings of Jesus in 5:16[22] or 6:2, and Luke openly portrays Jesus as being glorified by everyone (Luke 4:15; compare Matt 4:23; Mark 1:39).[23]

With regard to supplicatory and epiphanic worship, we note that nine of the ten reported instances present Jesus as the recipient (2:11; 8:2; 9:18; 14:33; 15:25; 20:20; 21:16; 28:9, 17). All nine of these instances, furthermore, are unique to Matthew's Gospel. Outside of Matthew, the Synoptic Gospels contain only three references to Jesus being worshiped and these are all passages that would seem out of place in Matthew. Mark's references to Jesus being worshiped (*proskyneō*) by a demon-possessed person (5:6, par Matt 8:28-34) and by blatantly insincere soldiers (15:9, par Matt 27:29) envision "worship" as formal action apart from attitude. Luke's reference to Jesus being glorified (*doxazō*) by all (4:15, par Matt 4:23) violates Matthew's desire to depict Jesus as one who does good works for the glory of God. If the absence of these three references is understandable within Matthew's narrative, the occurrence of the nine unique reports of Jesus being worshiped in Matthew is all the more impressive. We must conclude that the worship of Jesus is a much more pronounced theme in Matthew than in the other Synoptic Gospels.

This emphasis can be viewed as problematic because, in Matthew, Jesus himself declares that God is the only one who should be worshiped (4:10). With regard to supplicatory worship, this apparent difficulty is traditionally explained by saying that this type of worship involves no more than the sort of respect that one human being can appropriately show to another.[24] Such an explanation often appeals to 18:26, where the slave is said to wor-

---

22. For a potential non-Synoptic parallel to Matt 5:16, see John 15:8.

23. In Luke 17, a leper healed by Jesus glorifies God (17:15) *and* gives thanks to Jesus (17:16), although he is commended only for the former (17:18).

24. Peterson, e.g., takes *proskyneō* in 8:2; 9:18; 15:25; and 20:20 as "a form of homage and entreaty" that should not be viewed as worship (p. 85).

ship his king. This king, however, is explicitly identified as a
parabolic image of God (18:35), and, in any case, the slave who
worships him provides such a negative example that his action
cannot be taken as illustrative of what is appropriate. Moreover,
we have seen that in Matthew supplicatory worship implies a relationship in which the supplicant demonstrates total dependence on and confidence in the one who is worshiped. According
to Matthew, such relationships should never exist between
human beings (20:25-26; 23:10).

In any case, all five instances of epiphanic worship reported in
Matthew also portray Jesus as the recipient, and in these cases the
worship cannot possibly be construed as a demonstration of respect that one might show to a human being. Rather, this is precisely the type of worship that Jesus tells Satan is to be reserved
for God alone (4:10). Yet, Jesus does not reprove those who worship him in Matthew's narrative or remind them of the scripture
that he quoted to the devil. Apparently Jesus is to be regarded as
an exception to the otherwise absolute restriction of worship to
God. But why?

The rationale for this exception must lie in Matthew's Christology. The point that Jesus establishes in the last episode of the
temptation account (4:8-10) is not merely that the devil is unworthy of worship but that God alone is worthy of worship. According to this position, not only worship of devils is rejected but also
worship of angels or kings or prophets or messiahs. If Jesus qualifies for worship, it is not because he is any of these things but
because he is the Son of God (3:17; 14:33; 16:16; 27:54). He is
Emmanuel, the one in whom and through whom God is present
(1:23). Matthew does not explicitly attribute divinity to Jesus, but
by presenting Jesus as an appropriate recipient of worship Matthew does, for all practical purposes, portray Jesus as divine. God
is present in Jesus to such a degree that worship of Jesus counts as
worship of God.

Still, if Matthew's rationale for commending the worship of
Jesus lies in his christological understanding of Jesus as the Son
of God, we must recognize that such an understanding cannot be
attributed to the characters who are described as worshiping
Jesus in Matthew's story. The Magi, for instance, worship Jesus
simply because they believe he is a divinely ordained king of the
Jews (2:2). According to Matthew's own thinking, divinely or-

dained kings do not deserve worship (4:10). The story works, then, only when accounts of Jesus receiving worship are read at a level of understanding shared between the implied author and readers. Matthew's readers are expected to realize that such worship is appropriate for reasons that the Magi and other worshipers in the narrative do not themselves understand.

POSTSCRIPT:
WORSHIP AND TEACHING

The preceding comments concerning worshipers and recipients of worship in Matthew lead us to note a paradox in Matthew's portrayal of worship that may serve as a segue into our next chapter.

On the one hand, Matthew seems to present worship as an activity that precedes catechesis. Acceptable worship is engaged in by people of little faith (14:33; 28:17), by infants or children (21:16), and by pagan Gentiles (2:11; 15:31). Of those who worship Jesus, the only ones who do so with the recognition that he is the Son of God are his disciples, and both times when they do so their worship is explicitly associated with doubt (14:31-33; 28:17). Those who worship God may do so out of fear (9:8) or amazement (15:31) that lacks any real appreciation for what is going on. In short, Matthew does not present worship as activity appropriate only for the so-called "wise and intelligent" (11:25) but rather commends worship on the part of those who are theologically naive or immature.

On the other hand, Matthew's Gospel records Jesus as citing scriptures that denounce those who worship in vain, "teaching human precepts as doctrines" (15:9). This pronouncement forbids us to think that for Matthew sentiment or sincerity is what counts in worship even when doctrine is faulty. Worship that is not grounded in sound teaching will ultimately be in vain.

This paradoxical relationship between worship and teaching may be illustrated in Matthew's account of Jesus' entry to Jerusalem. As Jesus approaches the city he is greeted by crowds who acclaim, "Hosanna to the Son of David!" (21:9) and, later, when he enters the temple he is again greeted by children who say the same words (21:15). For Matthew, this confession of Jesus as the Son of David is correct but does not identify Jesus as one deserv-

ing of worship (4:10). As Jesus will indicate on his next visit to the
temple, he is not only David's son but also David's Lord (22:41-
45). "Whose son is the Christ?" he asks. Matthew's readers know
the answer: he is not only the son of David but also the son of
God, and the latter identification is what qualifies him to receive
worship.

The children in the temple who shout, "Hosanna to the Son
of David" do not know that Jesus is the Son of God, yet Jesus
describes their acclamation as divinely prepared praise (21:16).
Children in Matthew may serve as paradigms of the uninstructed, of those who are dependent on God (11:25) and others
(18:6) for enlightenment. Worship that gives expression to an
immature or incomplete understanding is appropriate for those
who are themselves immature and in need of instruction. Thus,
Jesus' commendation of the children's worship may illustrate one
half of the paradoxical relationship between worship and teaching in Matthew's Gospel, namely, that worship is a commendable
activity for the uninstructed.

The crowds who acclaim Jesus as the Son of David, however,
are treated quite differently. First, Matthew's Gospel carefully
distinguishes the crowds from the disciples in this account so that
readers may know that only the crowds and not the disciples
shout "Hosanna to the Son of David!" (21:9; compare Mark
11:9; Luke 19:37). Second, Matthew does not present Jesus as ap-
proving of the crowds' acclamation in any way whatsoever (compare Luke 19:39-40). And, finally, in verses unique to this
Gospel, Matthew describes the crowds as responding to those
who ask, "Who is this?" with the confident assertion, "This is
the prophet Jesus from Nazareth in Galilee" (21:10-11). By this
point in the story, Matthew's readers know that any designation
of Jesus as a mere prophet is shortsighted (16:13-17). Thus, Matthew calls attention to the inadequate basis for the crowds' acclaim and in this way prepares readers for later developments in
the narrative. Although the crowds ostensibly use the same words
that Jesus finds commendable on the lips of children, before the
week is through they will change their shouts of "Hosanna!" to
cries of "Crucify him!" They will even seek to implicate, specifically, their *children* in accepting responsibility for Jesus' blood
(27:22-25). Thus these crowds may be contrasted with the children in the temple to illustrate the other half of the paradoxical

relationship between worship and teaching in Matthew's Gospel. In their case, inadequate understanding, coupled with false confidence and presumption (21:10-11), produces acclamations that prove empty. In short, Matthew believes that worship is appropriate and commendable for the uninstructed but also regards worshiping communities as having a strong need of catechesis if their worship is not ultimately to be in vain. So, we should not be surprised to find the conclusion of this Gospel bringing the two themes of worship and teaching together under the overriding rubric of mission. When Jesus' disciples gather to worship him on the mountain in Galilee, they are sent out to make more disciples by teaching people to obey all of Jesus' commandments (28:17-20). This parting image of worshipers who teach what Jesus commanded presents a stark contrast to the earlier portrait of so-called worshipers who teach the precepts of humans (15:9). The worship of disciples whose teaching is defined by the commands of God's Son will not be in vain but will be sustained by the continuing presence of the one who has all authority in heaven and on earth.

CHAPTER THREE

TEACHING

THE CONCLUSION OF MATTHEW'S GOSPEL is well known. The risen Jesus meets with his eleven remaining disciples on a mountain in Galilee and commissions them to make disciples of all nations by baptizing people in the name of the Father, Son, and Holy Spirit and teaching them to obey all that Jesus has commanded (28:19-20).

What is less well known perhaps is that this passage is Matthew's only direct reference to the post-Easter teaching ministry of the church. If this passage were lacking, we might suppose that Matthew does not envision Jesus' followers as engaged in teaching at all. Jesus' own ministry is succinctly described in Matthew as teaching, preaching, and healing (4:23; 9:35; 11:1), but when Jesus sends his disciples out on mission, he tells them only to preach the gospel and heal the sick (10:7-8). Teaching is conspicuously absent from their job description. Again, in 23:8-10, Jesus explicitly forbids his followers to let themselves be called "rabbi," "father," or "instructor" (*kathēgētēs*).

Still, Matthew 28:20 makes clear that teaching is to be an important part of the ongoing work of Jesus' followers. Indeed, it is one of the most important aspects of the post-Easter mission, for teaching is the means by which the baptized are "made disciples" and the Great Commission is fulfilled. This disclosure in the final verse of the Gospel invites Matthew's readers to reconsider the preceding narrative with particular interest in the ministry of teaching to which the church is now committed.[1] When we accept this invitation we find that the Gospel actually

1. A book by Paul Minear attempts to do precisely this, to consider the whole of Matthew's Gospel as a volume dedicated to "basic educational work

has much to say that is relevant for carrying out Jesus' final directive.

As we attempt to read Matthew's narrative in light of its concluding commission, we may pay special attention to three questions: What is to be taught? To whom? And by whom? According to Matthew 28:20, the commandments of Jesus are to be taught to those who have been baptized by Jesus' disciples. Early on in this Gospel, however, Jesus offers some words on teaching that supply different answers to these questions. In 5:19 he declares, "Whoever breaks one of the least of these commandments [in the law], and teaches others to do the same, will be called least in the kingdom of heaven; but whoever does them and teaches them will be called great in the kingdom of heaven." The two passages may be summarized as follows:

	5:19	28:20
What is taught?	the law	Jesus' commands
To whom?	people	the baptized
By whom?	whoever	disciples

The first passage speaks generically in language that would be traditional for the Jewish milieu. The second passage uses language that is more specific for the Christian church. Scholars have sometimes sought to resolve a supposed tension between these passages by imposing some scheme of salvation-historical dispensations on Matthew's narrative, such that 5:19 may be read as applicable only for the time period before Easter and 28:20 as applicable for the era of the church after Easter. Such attempts run aground on Jesus' insistence in 5:18 that the commandments of the law will remain in full force until "heaven and earth pass away."[2] Nothing in Matthew indicates that 28:20 is intended to

---

among adult believers in Jesus Christ." See Paul S. Minear, *Matthew: The Teacher's Gospel* (New York: Pilgrim Press, 1982).

2. The most famous such attempt is that of John Meier, who would have us believe that heaven and earth do pass away, metaphorically, at the death and resurrection of Jesus, when all authority in heaven and on earth is given to him (28:18). See John P. Meier, *The Vision of Matthew* (TI; New York: Paulist Press, 1979), 229–34. But for Matthew the eventual demise of heaven and earth is a literal and still future event (24:29-44).

supplant 5:19 or that the latter is to be regarded as no longer having real significance for readers of the Gospel. We do better to take 28:20 as our source for the most clear and explicit definition of the teaching ministry of the church while remembering that 5:19 speaks also of teaching in terms that may both inform and transcend the mission of the church.

With this in mind, we may take up the three questions posed above in more detail.

WHAT IS TO BE TAUGHT?

According to both 5:19 and 28:20 the content of teaching is to be ethical. The focus is on *commandments*; no mention is made of what we would call doctrine. Elsewhere, of course, Jesus' followers are told to preach (*kerussō*) the good news of the kingdom (24:14; compare 10:7) and to confess (*homologeō*) Jesus (10:32), and we might assume that such proclamation implies instruction on eschatological and christological themes. Furthermore, if the teaching in 28:20 is indeed directed to the baptized, we may wonder how these candidates for discipleship came to be baptized in the first place. Surely representatives from "all nations" cannot be expected to be baptized in the name of the Father, Son, and Holy Spirit without first wanting to know, "Who is the Father?" "Who is the Son?" "Who or what is the Holy Spirit?" and, for that matter, "What is baptism?" Still, if logic dictates that the mission of the church envisioned by Matthew must include some sort of doctrinal instruction, we must grant that this component of the church's mission is not the focus of Matthew's Gospel. Matthew is more interested in the process of ethical formation by which those who have been baptized are made disciples.

This preeminent concern with ethics is consistent with the representation of the teaching of Jesus in Matthew's Gospel. Although Matthew says many times that Jesus teaches,[3] he rarely provides us with the content of this teaching. In Mark's Gospel, by contrast, instances in which Jesus teaches (*didaskō*) include predictions of his passion (Mark 8:31; 9:31, par Matt 16:21; 17:22) and sayings concerning the temple (Mark 11:17-18, par

3. See 4:23; 5:2; 7:28; 9:35; 11:1; 13:54; 21:23; 22:33; 26:55.

Matt 21:13) and the Son of David (Mark 12:35, par Matt 22:42). Mark also describes as teaching (*didachē*) Jesus' parable of the Sower (Mark 4:2, par Matt 13:3) and his denunciation of the ostentatious behavior of the scribes (Mark 12:38, par Matt 23:2-7). Although all of the passages just noted have parallels in Matthew's Gospel, Matthew invariably reports these words simply as things that Jesus said (*legō*, 17:22; 21:13; 22:42; 23:2) or spoke (*laleō*, 13:3) or showed (*deiknymi*, 16:21) to people. With one exception (22:33), Matthew does not use the word "teaching" (*didachē*) for sayings of Jesus in general but reserves that word for references to material that has strong ethical content (7:28-29; see also 5:2). For example, Matthew never presents Jesus as teaching in parables (compare Mark 4:2), because, while parables may reveal mysteries of the kingdom of heaven (13:10-11), Matthew does not regard such revelations as definitive of what was the *teaching* ministry of Jesus or of what should be the teaching ministry of the church.

The only instance where Matthew provides a sustained account of what he calls the "teaching" (*didachē*) of Jesus (7:28-29; see also 5:2) is in chapters 5–7, the three chapters popularly known as the Sermon on the Mount. Here Jesus tells people how to do the will of God so that they may enter the kingdom of heaven (7:21). First, Jesus insists, people must obey the commandments of the law, including those that are considered to be "the least" of the commandments (5:17). But to do God's will perfectly (5:48), superficial observance of the law's demands is not enough. Hence, Jesus interprets the law in ways that reveal what God truly desires: purity in thought (5:28) and word (5:22) as well as deed; sincere piety that is not just for show (6:1-6, 16-18); a lifestyle that reflects trust in God's providence (6:19-21, 24-34); and so on. Thus, Jesus begins by demanding obedience to the law but ends by saying a sure foundation also requires obedience to his words concerning the law (7:24-27).

Against this background, we may describe what Matthew envisions to be the content of the church's teaching in three categories:

1. The teaching of the church is to include *all the commandments of the law* (5:17-19). Twice in Matthew's Gospel, Jesus offers ethical summaries that capture the essence of the law's demands: "Do to others as you would have them do to you" (7:12)

and, Love God and neighbor (22:37-40). At other times, he indicates that some matters are more important than others (5:19; 9:13; 12:7; 23:23). Such statements provide hermeneutical guidance for interpretation of the law but do not imply that attention to the details of the law is no longer necessary. Rather, these statements are balanced by Jesus' insistence that every letter (*iota*) and stroke (*keraia*) of the law will remain in effect until heaven and earth pass away (5:18). Thus, the church is to obey and teach all of the commandments of the law, including "the least" (5:19).

2. The church is to teach *obedience to all that Jesus has commanded* (28:20). The use of the aorist in 28:20 (*eneteilamēn*) indicates that Matthew regards the teaching of Jesus as historically complete. The church is not to teach new commands given by the risen Jesus through spirit-filled prophets but is to teach what Jesus commanded during his earthly life. However, the word used here for "commanded" (*entellomai*) is only used once in Matthew to describe a specific directive of Jesus and then the reference is to a temporally conditioned matter no longer applicable to Matthew's readers (17:9).[4] Thus, the mention of what Jesus "has commanded" in 28:20 must be taken in a broad sense as referring to the ethical instruction of Jesus provided throughout the narrative. In particular, the church is to teach the words of Jesus concerning the law so that those who hear them and do them may have a sure foundation for doing the will of God and entering the kingdom of heaven (7:21-27).

Matthew's placement of the mandate to teach what Jesus has commanded in the postresurrection commission that concludes his narrative gives special prominence to this component of the church's teaching. Indeed, the words of Jesus do have preeminence over those of Moses for Matthew, since the former will remain even *after* heaven and earth have passed away (24:35; compare 5:18). But Matthew is careful to affirm this preeminence of Jesus' words while maintaining that Jesus has not come to abolish the law (5:17). At times Jesus may appear to overturn sayings of Moses in Matthew's Gospel (for example, 5:38-39 or

4. The word *entellomai* is used three times to refer to the commands of God (or Moses) in the scriptures (4:6; 15:4; 19:7). Likewise *entolē* ("commandment") is used only six times in Matthew, always in reference to the Mosaic law (5:19; 15:13; 19:17; 22:36, 38, 40).

19:7-9), but Matthew presents these as instances in which Jesus is interpreting the law in ways that fulfill its true intent. Rabbis often modified the literal sense of the law without being accused of abrogating it.[5] Accordingly, Matthew's readers are expected to perceive Jesus' adjustments to the Mosaic law as clarifications of the will of God to which that law attests.[6]

Notably, the church is not simply to teach people the commands of Jesus but is to teach people *to obey* what Jesus has commanded. The teaching ministry of the church is not just a matter of passing on information regarding what Jesus said but is definitively marked by an insistence that Jesus' words be heeded. The law as interpreted by Jesus offers the way to life, which is admittedly hard (7:13). Still, the requirements of Jesus may paradoxically be described as an easy yoke or a light burden (11:29), a designation that invites comparison with the "heavy burdens" that other interpreters of the law force their followers to bear (23:4). The way of Jesus is not easier because his legal interpretations are more lax (5:17-48; 19:3-9) but because it provides rest for the soul (11:29).

3. The church is to exercise the teaching function of *binding and loosing* (16:19; 18:18). The phrase "to bind and to loose" refers to the rabbinic activity of discerning the will of God for the present day by determining how commandments of the law apply in contemporary situations.[7] To "loose" a commandment in this sense must be distinguished from the activity of those who loose commandments in ways that mark them as least in the kingdom of heaven (5:19). Although the same Greek word (*lyō*) is used in 5:19; 16:19; and 18:18, context determines that the term carries a different nuance in the first of these instances. In 5:19, to loose a commandment means to abolish a portion of the law (compare 5:17). In 16:19 and 18:18, to loose a commandment means to determine that a law does not apply to a given situation.

5. See Klyne Snodgrass, "Matthew and the Law," in *SBL 1988 Seminar Papers*, ed. David S. Lull (Atlanta: Scholars Press, 1988), 536–54, esp. 549; *idem*, "Matthew's Understanding of the Law," *Int* 46 (1992): 368–78.

6. Morna H. Hooker, *Continuity and Discontinuity: Early Christianity in Its Jewish Setting* (London: Epworth Press, 1986), 31.

7. See chap. 1, n. 36 above.

Jesus himself exemplifies this activity in his own interpretation of the law. An example of binding a commandment would be his declaration that the law prohibiting adultery applies even to lustful thoughts (5:27-28). An example of loosing a commandment would be his decision that the law forbidding work on the Sabbath does not apply to picking grain to satisfy one's hunger (12:1-7). The church that Jesus builds (16:18) and sustains by his continuing presence (18:20) is authorized to continue this activity. In doing so, the church will bind and loose commandments of the law in keeping with the teaching of Jesus, which not only offers specific examples of legal interpretation but also provides hermeneutical guidance with regard to how such interpretation is to be done (7:12; 9:13; 12:7; 22:37-40; 23:23). Furthermore, since the words of Jesus concerning the law have now come to be regarded as commandments themselves (28:20), we may reasonably assume that they will also need to be interpreted. As ever new situations arise, the church will have to exercise its teaching function of binding and loosing with regard to the commands of Jesus as well as with regard to those of the law proper. Thus, even though the church is not to produce new commands of Jesus, neither is the content of its teaching to be limited to historical exposition. The church is expected to teach the will of God for the present as determined by its interpretation and understanding of what Jesus and the law commanded in the past.

TO WHOM IS TEACHING DIRECTED?

The audience that Matthew envisions for the teaching ministry of the church is potentially broad and inclusive. In 5:19, Jesus speaks of teaching "people" (*anthropoi*), and in 28:19-20 he commissions his disciples to teach "the nations" (*ta ethnē*). In both cases, the choice of words denotes a larger field than the "lost sheep of the house of Israel" to whom Jesus' disciples direct their original mission of preaching and healing (10:5-6). For Matthew, the will of God revealed through the law and through the teaching of Jesus is not a cultural phenomenon for a particular ethnic or social group but universal truth that should be taught to all human beings.

At the same time, Matthew's Gospel recognizes that the actual audience for the church's teaching will be restricted and fairly well defined. Most of this teaching will be directed to people from all nations who have been baptized in the name of the Father, Son, and Holy Spirit (28:16-20). Thus, the audience for the church's teaching may be diverse culturally and ethnically, but it will be united by the common identity assumed through baptism and by the confessions and commitments this implies. For Matthew, the teaching of the church is primarily concerned with ethical formation and this is to take place within the community of faith rather than in the world at large.

This perspective on teaching colors Matthew's presentation of Jesus' ministry. Jesus is never described as teaching "the crowds" in Matthew's Gospel, although the Gospel of Mark says he does this customarily (Mark 10:1; see also 2:13; 4:1). Rather, Jesus does most of his teaching in the synagogues (4:23; 9:35; 13:34) or in the temple (21:23; 26:55), that is, in locations where the audience would already have some prior commitment to a faith community. The sole reference in Matthew to Jesus teaching "in their cities" (11:1) is probably meant to imply that he taught in the synagogues of those various cities rather than in the public squares.

Neither the teaching of Jesus nor that of the church is to be reserved for faith communities because of any inherent esoteric quality. On the contrary, the content of this teaching is universal truth from which all people can potentially benefit. But from a practical standpoint, teaching that is intended to fulfill the law (5:17) or make disciples (28:19) is wasted on those who have no commitment to keeping the law or becoming disciples. Thus, Jesus advises his followers, "Do not give what is holy to dogs; and do not throw your pearls before swine, or they will trample them under foot and turn and maul you" (7:6). The teaching ministry of the church must be primarily internal because, Matthew imagines, the baptized will listen to the commandments of Jesus in a way that the world will not. Still, the universal truth of Jesus' teaching is affirmed through the claim that if people in the world at large were to heed these commandments, they would benefit from them. Jesus goes on to say, "*Everyone. . .* who hears these words of mine and acts on them will be like a wise man who built his house on rock" (7:24).

This paradoxical vision of the church teaching internally what is potentially of value to the less receptive world outside can be illustrated with regard to the Sermon on the Mount, from which both of the passages quoted in the paragraph above derive (7:6, 24). Scholars have long noted that this Sermon presents ethical standards for the community of faith. Matthew's readers are expected to accept what Jesus says in chapters 5–7 not because it makes sense or rings true existentially but because Jesus himself is the authoritative agent of God. Descended from Abraham and David (1:1), he was begotten by the Holy Spirit (1:20) and born of a virgin (1:25). He is the Messiah (1:1), the one spoken of by the prophets (1:22; 2:6, 15, 18, 23; 3:14). His authoritative status is recognized by angels (1:20; 2:13) and by devils (4:1-11), by Herod (2:3) and by John the Baptist (3:11-14), by gentile Magi (2:1-2) and by Jewish priests (2:4-6). Even God has declared from heaven that "this is my Son, the Beloved, with whom I am well pleased" (3:17). When such a person "opens his mouth" (5:2), we ought to pay attention to what he says—whether it makes sense to us or not! In short, Matthew's Gospel assumes that acceptance of Jesus' ethical teaching is predicated on prior acceptance of the christological doctrine expounded in the narrative.

The same may be said of eschatology. The Sermon on the Mount is presented in Matthew as an explication of Jesus' basic message: "Repent, for the kingdom of heaven has come near" (4:17). In chapters 5–7, Jesus teaches what it means to "repent," and the assumption throughout is that the repentance he describes is undergirded by a recognition that the kingdom of heaven is near. Refusing to retaliate against one's enemies (5:38-39), to accumulate wealth (6:19), and to be concerned about what one will eat, drink, or wear (6:25) are viewed as wise courses of action (7:24-25) only in light of the rewards and reversals that the eschatological kingdom will bring.

Nevertheless, centuries of interpretation have revealed that many people do appreciate the Sermon on the Mount for its ethical teaching alone, apart from the christological and eschatological basis that Matthew provides. To cite a famous example, Thomas Jefferson rejected the doctrinal claims of Christian communities (Christology and eschatology in particular!) but treasured the Sermon on the Mount as a paradigm of instruction in virtue and morality. Matthew's Gospel seems to anticipate the possibility of such a response through its presentation of Jesus' words as universal truth for all humanity.

This ambiguity of audience is expressed explicitly within the text of Matthew's Gospel itself. At the beginning of the Sermon, Matthew clearly indicates that these words are spoken by Jesus to his disciples apart from the crowds (5:1-2). But at the Sermon's end, we are suddenly told that the crowds are astonished at his teaching, which they have apparently overheard (7:28; compare 22:33). Astonishment, of course, is a neutral reaction that implies neither acceptance nor rejection.[8] This image of Jesus instructing his disciples while astonished crowds "listen in" offers a paradigm for the audiences Matthew envisions for the church's teaching. The church's task is not to instruct the world with regard to morality but to make disciples of the baptized (28:20). Rather than casting its pearls before swine (7:6), the church ought to concentrate on teaching committed members of the community to obey the will of God as explicated in the law (5:19) and in the commandments of Jesus (28:20). Still, the message with which the church is entrusted is so inherently authoritative (7:29; 28:18) that the church should not be surprised to find that these words make an impression on those outside the community as well.

WHO IS TO TEACH?

The question of who has authority to teach is addressed in Matthew's Gospel in two ways, with reference to Jesus and the religious leaders of Israel on the one hand and with reference to Jesus and his own disciples on the other. With regard to the religious leaders, the emphasis seems to be on circumscribing teaching authority, on leading readers to recognize who does *not* have authority to teach. With regard to the disciples, the emphasis appears to be on reducing restrictions, on leading readers to accept a generous understanding of who has authority to teach. These tendencies should not be viewed as antithetical. Taken together, they indicate that parameters exist, although they are broad.

Jesus and the Religious Leaders.   In Matthew's story, Jesus and the religious leaders are presented as competitors, both claiming to have authority to teach. The religious leaders actu-

8. See above, p. 41.

ally represent various groups (Pharisees, Saduccees, scribes, priests, elders) but, in Matthew, are generally lumped together and treated as a single entity (16:12).[9]

The conflict is foreshadowed in the infancy narrative of Matthew's Gospel when Herod summons the chief priests and scribes of the people and asks them where the Messiah is to be born. They know the answer and they tell him (2:5), setting in motion an attempt to kill Jesus and precipitating a massacre of infants (2:16-17). Matthew's readers may note even at this early stage of the narrative that the religious leaders have knowledge of scripture but that this knowledge is used to further evil purposes rather than the purposes of God.

In the Sermon on the Mount, Jesus emerges as a teacher in his own right (5:2), and the contrast between his teaching and that of the religious leaders is made explicit. In his teaching, Jesus articulates and insists on a way of righteousness that fulfills the law and the prophets (5:17) and leads to greatness in the kingdom of heaven (5:19). Some teachers, Jesus avers, are prone to relax the commandments of the law and these teachers as well as their followers will be least in the kingdom of heaven (5:19). But the scribes and the Pharisees exemplify something much worse—if one's righteousness does not exceed that of the scribes and the Pharisees, one will not enter the kingdom of heaven at all (5:20).

Interpreters of Matthew's Gospel sometimes take this declaration by Jesus to mean that the righteousness *exhibited* by disciples must exceed that *exhibited* by the scribes and the Pharisees. The context of Matthew 5:20, however, implies more than this. In the preceding verses Jesus is emphasizing what one "does and teaches." We should assume, therefore, that according to Jesus the righteousness *exhibited and demanded* by the scribes and the Pharisees is insufficient for admission to the kingdom of heaven. This view is consistent with what follows in the Sermon on the Mount, where Jesus contrasts his own stringent demands with traditional, relatively lax interpretations (5:21-48).

9. On Matthew's presentation of the religious leaders as a unified "character group," see Jack Dean Kingsbury, "The Developing Conflict between Jesus and the Jewish Leaders in Matthew's Gospel: A Literary-Critical Study," *CBQ* 49 (1987): 57–73.

To say, however, that the teaching of the scribes and the Pharisees is wrong because it is too lax is to tell only part of the story. Later in this narrative, readers will encounter instances where the interpretations of the scribes and the Pharisees are too stringent (12:1-8, 9-12; 23:4). Thus, the teaching of the religious leaders in Matthew is consistently wrong, but it is not wrong in a consistent way. They "bind" what should be loosed and they "loose" what should be bound.

A clue for identifying the basic problem with the religious leaders' teaching is provided at the conclusion of the Sermon on the Mount. When Jesus finishes speaking, the crowds are astonished at his teaching. Why? Because, Matthew explains, Jesus' teaching comes from one who has authority, whereas the teaching that the crowds are accustomed to hearing—that of their scribes—comes from people who do not have authority (7:28-29).[10] In order to grasp the significance of this explanation, we must note the point of view that is here expressed. Matthew does not say that the crowds are astonished by Jesus' teaching because they perceive that he teaches with authority. We do not know yet whether the crowds perceive Jesus as having authority or not (but see 9:8). Rather, the explanation for the crowds' astonishment is offered by Matthew himself, that is, by the narrator of the Gospel story. In a narrative such as this one, intrusive comments by the narrator are intended to provide readers with important inside information for making sense of the story.[11] In other words, from this point in the story on, Matthew's readers are expected to know something that the characters in the story may or may not know, namely, that Jesus has authority to teach

---

10. A number of commentators take this passage as merely expressing a contrast between the unique teaching style of Jesus and the traditional methods of the rabbis. See W. F. Albright and C. S. Mann, *Matthew* (AB 26; Garden City, N.Y.: Doubleday & Co., 1971), 88–89; Francis W. Beare, *The Gospel according to Matthew* (San Francisco: Harper & Row, 1981), 200; Robert H. Gundry, *Matthew: A Commentary on His Literary and Theological Art* (Grand Rapids: Wm. B. Eerdmans, 1982), 137; and David Hill, *The Gospel of Matthew* (NCB; Grand Rapids: Wm. B. Eerdmans, 1972), 155–56. Such an interpretation takes the participial phrase (*hōs exousian echōn*) circumstantially to mean "authoritatively." While grammatically possible, this reading fails to convey that from the narrator's perspective the authority of Jesus is not only apparent but real.

11. Powell, *Narrative Criticism*, 25–27.

while the religious leaders of Israel do not.[12] Thus, the essential problem with the religious leaders' teaching is defined not as a problem of *content* but as a problem of *authority*.

As Matthew's story continues, Jesus will claim to have authority in other areas as well, always in contexts where he is challenged by the religious leaders. He claims, for instance, to have authority on earth to forgive sins (9:6) and to reform the temple (21:12-13, 23-27). Ultimately, he will claim to have been given all authority in heaven and on earth (28:17). The religious leaders, by contrast, are shown to be evil persons (9:4; 12:34, 39, 45; 16:4; 22:18) who have reneged on whatever responsibilities God once entrusted to them and, in their rebellion against God, have seized for themselves prerogatives God never intended them to have (21:33-45). In fact, they are like "plants" that the "heavenly Father has not planted" (15:13), like tares sown by the devil in God's field of wheat (13:24-25, 37-39).

The contest of authority between Jesus and these religious leaders is central to the entire plot of Matthew's Gospel, and this contest is played out first and perhaps foremost with regard to teaching. The point that Matthew wishes to make with regard to the religious leaders is not simply that their teaching is wrong. The point, rather, is that they have no authority to teach in the first place. For Matthew, then, "false teachers" are not fundamentally people whose teaching is false but people who teach when they are not authorized to teach. The distinction is significant because, as the episode with Herod (2:3-6) reveals, false teachers may promote what is evil even when the content of their teaching is superficially correct. As people who have no authority to teach, the religious leaders are represented in Matthew as people whose teaching is not only wrong but dangerous (16:12). It does not lead people to God's kingdom but causes people to fall into a pit (15:14) or to become children of hell (23:15).

12. What is said here of the scribes holds equally for all of the religious leaders in Matthew, for the scribes are associated with the chief priests and the elders (16:21; 20:18; 21:15; 26:57; 27:41) and with the Pharisees (5:20; 12:38; 15:1; 23:2, 13, 14, 15, 23, 25, 27, 29) who in turn are linked with the Sadducees (3:7; 16:1, 6, 11, 12; see also 27:62).

EXCURSUS: MATTHEW 23:2-7

One passage in Matthew's Gospel seems to contradict the points we have just made. We must examine this passage at length, for its interpretation has great bearing on Matthew's concept of teaching.[13]

In Matthew 23:2-7, Jesus tells his disciples that "the scribes and the Pharisees sit on Moses' seat." Therefore the disciples should do (*poieō*) and keep (*tēreō*) whatever these religious leaders say (*legō*) to them, but the disciples should not do (*poieō*) according to the works (*erga*) of these leaders. Why? Because the scribes and the Pharisees speak (*legō*) but do not do (*poieō*), burden people whom they are unwilling to help, and do (*poieō*) all their deeds (*erga*) to be seen by others. Traditional readings[14] have taken this passage as affirming three things. First, by saying that the scribes and the Pharisees "sit on Moses' seat," Jesus grants that they have authority to interpret the scriptures for God's people. They have authority to "bind and loose," to determine on the basis of the scriptures what is the will of God for present circumstances. Second, by telling his disciples to do and keep whatever the scribes and the Pharisees say, Jesus commends adherence to the teaching of these religious leaders. Jesus' followers ought to respect the authority of these teachers and live in accordance with their interpretations of scripture. Third, by telling his disciples not to do "according to their works," Jesus indicates that the real flaw these religious leaders exhibit is that they do not live in accord with their own teaching. Thus, by following the teaching of the scribes and the Pharisees, Jesus' disciples will fulfill the will of God to a degree that the scribes and the Pharisees themselves do not.

As most scholars are willing to grant, this interpretation holds only when Matthew 23:2-7 is considered as an isolated pericope, apart from its context within Matthew as a whole.[15] If the sense of

13. For a fuller discussion, see Mark Allan Powell, "Do and Keep What Moses Says (Matthew 23:2-7)," forthcoming in *JBL*.

14. For a summary of representative views, see David E. Garland, *The Intention of Matthew 23* (NovTSup 52; Leiden: E. J. Brill, 1979). Garland's own analysis is insightful but fails to resolve the problems noted here.

15. This tension is usually resolved source-critically under the assumption that the Gospel's redactor has incorporated here a tradition at variance with his own preferred stance. See Stephenson H. Brooks, *Matthew's Community: The Evidence of His Special Sayings Source* (JSNTSS 16; Sheffield: JSOT Press,

these verses was extended to a consideration of the entire narrative, we would be left with a bizarre picture indeed. We would
have to assume that the teaching of the scribes and the Pharisees
concerning such matters as the Sabbath (12:1-14), ritual hand
washings (15:1-2, 10-20), offerings (15:3-9), and divorce (15:3-9)
is correct.

Hence Jesus' disciples ought to refrain from plucking
grain or healing on the Sabbath, they ought to wash their hands
ritually before eating, they ought to feel free to give as a religious
offering money that would have been spent caring for their parents, and they ought to feel free to divorce their wives simply by
writing out the required certificates of divorce. Besides this, we
would also have to assume that the great failing of the scribes and
the Pharisees in these instances is that they do not follow their
own (correct) teaching. Apparently, they do pluck grain and perform healings on the Sabbath, they fail to wash their hands properly, they hold back for their parents what might have been given
as a religious offering, and they neglect to write certificates of divorce. But no sustained reading of Matthew would support these
conclusions. Obviously, in every instance cited, the problem is not
that the religious leaders do not follow their own teaching. The
problem is that the teaching itself is wrong.

In fact, the traditional interpretation of Matthew 23:2-7 con-
tradicts what is presented elsewhere in Matthew at every point.
First, Matthew's Gospel is not likely to present Jesus here as affirming the scribes' authority to teach when it has said elsewhere
that they do not have this authority (7:29). Second, Matthew's
Gospel is not likely to present Jesus here as commending adherence to the teaching of the Pharisees when elsewhere it presents
Jesus as warning his disciples to beware of their teaching (16:12;
see also 15:15; 23:14). And, finally, Matthew's Gospel is not likely
to present Jesus here as claiming that the religious leaders' flaw is

---

1987), 59–64, and the works listed by Brooks in note 3 on pp. 144–45. A few
scholars, however, argue that 23:2-3 betrays the redactor's own agenda, which is
to accept or revise Pharisaic *halacha*. Reinhardt Hummel, *Die Auseinanderset-
zung zwischen Kirche und Judentum im Matthäusevangelium* (BEvT 33; Munich:
Chr. Kaiser Verlag, 1966); and H. J. Schoeps, "Jésus et la loi juive," *RHPR* 33
(1953): 1–20. Some scholars attempt to explain Jesus' words in 23:2-3 as ironic
or rhetorical: Joachim Jeremias, *New Testament Theology: The Proclamation of
Jesus* (New York: Charles Scribner's Sons, 1971), 210; and Robert Banks, *Jesus
and the Law in Synoptic Tradition* (SNTSMS 28; Cambridge: Cambridge University Press, 1975), 176. See Powell, "Do and Keep," for a fuller discussion of
these and other ideas.

simply that they do not follow their own teaching when elsewhere it portrays Jesus as regarding them as godless agents of the devil (15:13; compare 13:37-39; 23:15) whose very thoughts and motives are evil (9:4; 12:39, 45; 16:4; 22:18) and whose words reflect this evil as clearly as their deeds (12:34).

The traditional interpretation of Matthew 23:2-7 is pervasive, even though it cannot be reconciled with the perspective of Matthew's Gospel as a whole. It is reflected in many English translations, where *legō* may curiously be translated "preach" (JB, NIV, NJB, RSV, TEV) or "teach" (NRSV). Such translations have contributed to a widespread notion of the Pharisees in Matthew as hypocrites who do not "practice what they preach." In fact, Matthew's Gospel never once portrays the Pharisees or any other religious leaders as failing to live according to their own teaching. Furthermore, Matthew's Gospel never defines hypocrisy as a discrepancy between word and deed but, rather, as a discrepancy between the inward nature observed by God and the outward appearance observed by others (23:25-28).[16] Words (22:15-18) and deeds (6:2) alike may present this false image, which apparently may be the product either of conscious pretense or unwitting self-deception.[17] Thus, a hypocrite may be one who does ostensibly good things with wrong motives (6:2, 5, 16), or who worships with lips but not with the heart (15:7-8), or who does good in trivial matters while neglecting important ones (23:23), or who presumes to minister to others without first correcting one's own failings (7:4-5; 23:13-15, 29-30). Also, in Matthew (15:7-9) and elsewhere (Gal 2:13; 1 Tim 4:1-2) hypocrisy is specifically related to false teaching.[18] But the popular notion of a hypocrite as someone who says one thing and does another has no support in Matthew's Gospel even though, ironically, it probably derives from mistranslations and misrepresentations of this Matthean text (23:2-3).

If we look at the passage more closely, we find that in Matthew 23:2-3 Jesus says that the scribes and the Pharisees do two things, one of which he commends and one of which he denounces. The

16. On hypocrisy in Matthew, see Sjef van Tilborg, *The Jewish Leaders in Matthew* (Leiden: E. J. Brill, 1972), 8–26; Garland, 91–123; and Dan O. Via, Jr., *Self-Deception and Wholeness in Paul and Matthew* (Minneapolis: Fortress Press, 1990), 92–98.

17. Van Tilborg stresses pretense and Via, self-deception. Garland correctly notes the presence of both.

18. Garland, 112–15.

commendable activity is referred to twice by the word *legō* ("speak") and is said to derive from their sitting on the seat of Moses. The activity that is denounced is referred to once by the phrase *ta erga autōn* ("their works") and once by the word *poieō* ("do"). Traditional readings of this passage have identified the first activity with teaching or interpretation of Mosaic law and the second activity with the lifestyle of those who teach or interpret the law. Even apart from the inconsistencies this causes for Matthew's narrative, these identifications are problematic because they assume a modern dichotomy that would be unlikely in a first-century Semitic document. In the world that produced Matthew's Gospel, teaching was never considered to be an activity that could be identified with speaking as opposed to doing. This world made no clear distinction between theory and praxis. The rabbis (including Jesus) taught their interpretations of Moses not merely by articulating their understanding of the law verbally but, above all, by living in ways that modeled this understanding. Thus, in Matthew's Gospel, Jesus contests the interpretations of the law offered by the scribes and the Pharisees not simply by arguing with them but primarily by doing things (such as healing on the Sabbath) that challenge their interpretation of Moses and endorse his own. In short, identification of "speaking" with teaching and "doing" with lifestyle in this passage violates not only the literary context of Matthew's narrative but also the dynamics of the social milieu in which this Gospel was produced.

Since the traditional interpretation of this passage is inadequate, I propose a different reading. My suggestion hinges on the possibility that when Jesus says the scribes and the Pharisees sit on Moses' seat he means that they are the keepers of the Torah, the ones who know and are able to tell others what Moses said. Cecil Roth and Kenneth Newport present arguments for regarding the "seat of Moses" as a literal piece of synagogue furniture, possibly the stand on which the law scroll itself rested.[19] But even if this is not the case and we are to take the phrase metaphori-

19. Cecil Roth, "The Chair of Moses and Its Survivals," *PEQ* 81 (1949): 100–111; and Kenneth G. C. Newport, "A Note on the 'Seat of Moses,' " *AUSS* 28 (1990): 53–58. Cf. Wilhelm Bacher, "Le Siège de Moïse," *REJ* 34 (1987): 229–301; E. L. Sukenik, *Ancient Synagogues in Palestine and Greece* (London: British Academy, 1934), 57–61; and M. Sulzberger, "Encore le Siège de Moïse," *REJ* 35 (1897): 110–11.

cally,[20] we need not assume that it is a metaphor for teaching authority. The most natural application would be to regard those who (metaphorically) sit on Moses' seat as those who speak Moses' words either by reading them from the scrolls themselves or by citing them from memory. Thus, those who occupy the seat of Moses (literally or metaphorically) may be regarded as those who control accessibility to Torah even if they are not regarded as persons who have the insight or authority to interpret Torah.

In saying that the scribes and the Pharisees sit on Moses' seat, Jesus may be simply acknowledging the powerful social and religious position they occupy in Matthew's story world, a world in which most people are illiterate and copies of the Torah are not plentiful.[21] Since Jesus' disciples do not themselves have copies of the Torah, they will be dependent on the scribes and the Pharisees to know what Moses said on any given subject.[22] In light of such dependence, Jesus advises his disciples to heed the words that the scribes and the Pharisees speak when they sit on the seat of Moses, that is, when they pass on the words of the Torah itself. The first activity of the scribes and the Pharisees, the one that Jesus commends, refers not to teaching or interpretation of Moses but simply to citation of Moses.[23]

The second activity of the scribes and the Pharisees, the one that Jesus denounces, refers to their interpretation of Moses through both verbal teaching and practiced lifestyle. Their works

20. M. Ginsburger, "La 'Chaire de Moise,' " *REJ* 90 (1931): 161–65; and Benedict T. Viviano, "Social World and Community Leadership: The Case of Matthew 23.1-12, 34," *JSNT* 39 (1990): 3–21.

21. Anthony Saldarini suggests that "Matthew is acknowledging either the official position of his opponents in the Jewish community or their influence on those in power." See Anthony J. Saldarini, "Delegitimation of Leaders in Matthew 23," *CBQ* 54 (1992): 659–80, esp. 670. My suggestion is compatible with this proposal, but more specific.

22. Notably, the only instance in Matthew that portrays the disciples as evincing knowledge of scripture represents them as citing information they have heard from "the scribes" (Matt 17:10).

23. An obvious forum for such citation would be public reading of scripture, but in Matthew's Gospel religious leaders often show themselves to be adept at citing Moses from memory (2:4-6; 19:7; 22:24). If the seat of Moses refers to an actual piece of synagogue furniture (see note 19 above), then formal public reading is probably the primary mode of citation intended by *legō* ("speak") in 23:3. Otherwise, the use of this term as opposed to *anaginōskō* ("read") suggests that speaking from the seat of Moses includes informal modes of citation as well.

(*ta erga autōn*) include the work of interpreting Moses. Jesus does not denounce them for acting in ways that contravene their own correct understanding of Torah but for acting in ways that reveal a perverted understanding of Torah. That this is the case is clear from the remainder of the passage. What the scribes and the Pharisees do (*poieō*) is interpret Moses in ways that are burdensome for others (23:4) and in ways that bring glory to themselves (23:5-7). Matthew's readers should not imagine, for instance, that the Pharisees correctly teach that phylacteries ought to be modest and then contradict their own teaching by wearing ostentatious phylacteries themselves (23:5). Rather, the scribes and the Pharisees demonstrate by their wearing of ostentatious phylacteries that they do not interpret the Mosaic injunction properly.

When Matthew 23:3 says that the scribes and the Pharisees "speak" (*legō*) but "do not do" (*poieō*), the implication is that they "speak Torah but do not do Torah." To "speak Torah" means to cite accurately what the scriptures say. To "do Torah" means to demonstrate understanding of Torah through word and deed (5:19). In Matthew's Gospel, Jesus claims that the scribes and the Pharisees do cite the Torah accurately, but he maintains that their words and their deeds reveal them to be "blind guides" who do not understand the Torah they cite (15:14, 23:16, 17, 19, 24, 26).

This interpretation of 23:2-7 not only respects the dynamics of the social milieu in which this Gospel was produced but also provides a reading consistent with the perspective of Matthew's narrative as a whole. Throughout this Gospel, the only thing that the religious leaders ever do right is quote scripture. The chief priests and the scribes know that the prophets identify Bethlehem as the birthplace of the Christ (2:4-6; see Mic 5:1-3), although they err in giving this information to Herod who seeks the child's life (2:16-18). The Pharisees know that Moses commanded the giving of divorce certificates (19:7; see Deut 24:1-4) but do not understand that this was due only to the hardness of their hearts (19:8-9). The Sadducees know that Moses said when a man dies childless his brother should marry the widow and raise up children for his brother (22:24; see Deut 25:5), but they do not "know the scriptures" in the broader sense of realizing that they teach a resurrection from the dead (22:29-32). The Pharisees know that the scriptures say the Christ is the son of David (22:42) but they do not understand that the Christ is also David's Lord (22:43-45). The chief priests know that it is unlawful to place blood money into the temple treasury (27:6; see Deut 23:18), but they have clearly missed the big picture by paying out blood money in the first place. On this point, Matthew's Gospel is consistent: the scribes, the Pharisees, and all of Israel's religious leaders may be commended only for knowing what scripture says, not for understanding what it means. We may note in this regard that Matthew also presents Satan as one who quotes scripture accurately, albeit with perverse intent (4:6; see Ps 91:11).

Our conclusion, then, is that Jesus' statement that the scribes and the Pharisees "sit on Moses' seat" is not intended as an endorsement of their authority to teach or interpret the law. Indeed, Jesus does not say that the scribes and the Pharisees *ought* to sit on Moses' seat or imply that their occupation of this position is a good thing. Rather, his statement merely acknowledges the reality of the situation in which his disciples must live and conduct their ministry. If they are to "do" (*poieō*) and "teach" (*didaskō*) the commandments (5:19), they must obviously know what Moses says. Since the scribes and the Pharisees are currently the keepers of the Torah in the social and religious environment where these disciples live, Jesus' followers must be careful to do (*poieō*) and obey (*tēreō*) all the words of Moses that they hear these leaders speak (*legō*). But in no case are they to copy what the scribes and the Pharisees do (*poieō*) with Moses, for what the scribes and the Pharisees do (*poieō*) and teach (*didaskō*) does not produce a righteousness that qualifies one for entrance to the kingdom of heaven (5:19-20). Why not? Because, in spite of the power of controlling accessibility to Torah that the scribes and the Pharisees now exercise, they do not in fact have authority to *teach* (7:29). Their understanding of the law and their actions that derive from and demonstrate this understanding are wrong, and must be wrong, for the authority they presume to possess has been given to another (7:28-29; 9:6-8; 12:8; 21:23-27; 28:18).

Jesus and His Disciples. From the Great Commission passage (28:16-20) we may surmise that authority to teach (as well as to baptize) is given to Jesus' eleven disciples, but we would be wrong to assume that Matthew projects an apostolic teaching office begun by them and passed on through time to others whom they appoint. For one thing, Matthew presents Jesus as commending "whoever" obeys the commandments and teaches them (5:19). For another, Matthew presents Jesus as explicitly telling his disciples that they are not to be called "rabbi" (23:8), they are to call no one "father," and they are not to be called "instructor" (*kathēgētēs*) (23:10). Matthew's readers are expected to know that these three terms (rabbi, father, and instructor) were all titles of honor for teachers of the law.[24] Elsewhere, Matthew's Gospel mentions prophets (10:41; 23:34), wise ones (23:34), righteous ones (10:41), little ones (10:42; compare 18:6, 10, 14), and scribes (13:52; 23:34) as being active among the community. We cannot be sure whether such terms designate offices within the church or are simply descriptive of functions or attributes for which some persons are noted.[25] But one thing is certain: the institution of a hierarchical *teaching* office is absolutely forbidden.

The reason for this prohibition is twofold. First, Jesus himself is to be the one teacher for all of his followers (23:8b). For another to assume such a position would create potential for a disciple being placed above the teacher, which Jesus says is not appropriate (10:24). Second, the disciples themselves are all siblings (*adelphoi*, 23:8c). For some to be officially recognized as teachers within the community would create potential for competition and status consciousness that would destroy the servant ethic that any community of Jesus' followers is to embrace (20:25-28).

The paradox, then, is that Jesus' followers are to make disciples by teaching (28:20), but they are not to designate any among them as "teachers" in an official or hierarchical sense. Is there a way to answer the question "Who is to teach?" that resolves this paradox? We might begin by inquiring into the qualifications of the eleven disciples whom Jesus commissions for teaching at the end of the Gospel. Since these eleven are not representative of a teaching office, might they rather be representative of *the sort of persons* who will conduct teaching ministries commissioned by Jesus as the church continues to make disciples of all nations?

At first blush, the disciples do not seem especially qualified for such a ministry. Throughout the Gospel, they show themselves to be persons of little faith (6:30; 8:26; 14:31; 16:8; 17:20), and they often fail Jesus by exhibiting behavior or attitudes that he finds displeasing (for example, 19:13-14; 20:20-28; 26:40-41).

24. J. D. M. Derrett, "Mt 23, 8-9 a Midrash on Is 54, 13 and Jer 31, 33-34," *Bib* 62 (1981): 372–86, esp. 377–81.

25. See Eduard Schweizer, "Matthew's Church," trans. Robert Morgan, in Stanton, *The Interpretation of Matthew*, 129–55.

Shortly before they receive their commission to teach, they desert Jesus in his hour of greatest need, sleeping when they ought to pray (26:36-45), fleeing in the face of danger (26:56), and denying knowledge of him altogether (26:59-75). Even at the time they receive the commission, their worship of Jesus is still mingled with doubt (28:17).

On closer examination, however, the disciples do seem to have two traits that qualify them for teaching the commands of Jesus. First, whatever may be said about their faith or faithfulness, they are at least persons who understand Jesus (13:51; 16:12; 17:13), persons who have ears that hear (13:16; compare 11:15; 13:9, 43). This is not to be taken lightly. In the parable of the Sower, Jesus compares the seed that falls on good soil and bears much fruit to those who hear the word and understand it (13:19, 23). Presumably, even cowards and doubters may be able to make disciples by teaching the word of Jesus if they themselves have heard this word and understood it.

The second thing that qualifies the disciples for teaching is the continuing presence of Jesus among them. The commission to teach is bracketed in Matthew's Gospel by Jesus' claim to have been given all authority in heaven and on earth (28:18) and by his promise to be with those he commissions to the close of the age (28:20). Thus, the disciples themselves do not have authority to teach, but the one who does possess this authority remains with them. They are his agents—whoever welcomes them, welcomes him (10:40).

If we consider these two qualifications for teaching within the context of Matthew's Gospel, we will realize that they are given inexplicably at the discretion of God and are potentially available to all members of Jesus' community. In Matthew's Gospel, the disciples understand Jesus not because of their native intelligence or educational background but because it is given to them "to know the secrets of the kingdom" (13:11). In fact, God delights in hiding things from the so-called "wise and intelligent" of this world, choosing instead to reveal them to "infants" (11:25-26). Likewise, the continuing presence of Jesus is no special prerogative of the eleven disciples. Jesus promises to be present wherever two or three gather in his name (18:20) and, again, claims that his presence will sometimes be hidden in unlikely guises (18:5; 25:31-46).

For Matthew, then, any member of the community who has understood the word of Jesus and with whom Jesus is present is authorized to teach others to obey the commands of Jesus. Such an egalitarian policy creates potential for the opposite problem that a hierarchical, status-conscious structure would bring. The problem now will be discernment between conflicting views within the community. In view of this problem, Matthew's Gospel offers three tests for determining whether a member of the community is teaching the commands of Jesus faithfully.

The first test is provided by the content of the Gospel itself. Matthew's Gospel offers not only a narrative account of Jesus' life but also an abundant record of his teaching. Thus, anyone who claims to be teaching what Jesus commanded ought to be teaching material consistent with the record of Jesus' ministry that Matthew provides.

This test could be applied easily on a superficial level to detect disparity in content between the claims of Jesus' followers and the actual teaching of Jesus recorded in Matthew's Gospel. For example, if anyone should claim that Jesus approved of divorce "for any cause," the claim could be immediately rejected by an appeal to Matthew 5:31-32 or 19:3-9. On a deeper level, the test could also be applied to disputes regarding interpretation of Jesus' commandments for the new situations that an ongoing mission to the nations will bring. Matthew's record of Jesus' teaching contains not only examples of specific instruction but also hermeneutical principles for determining how the law is to be fulfilled. These include the principles that one should treat others as one wishes to be treated (7:12), that God desires mercy over sacrifice (9:13; 12:7), that all the law and prophets depend on the commandments of love for God and neighbor (22:34-40), and that the weightier matters of the law are justice, mercy, and faith (23:23). Those who claim that their teaching represents an application of what Jesus commanded for the present day would be expected to justify their interpretation in light of principles such as these.

A second test Matthew's Gospel provides for determining the legitimacy of teaching within the community concerns the character of the person who teaches. According to an admittedly mixed metaphor in this Gospel, false prophets or "wolves in sheep's clothing" may be detected by their fruits (7:15-20; see also 12:33). Specifically, such persons fail to "do the will of the Father in heaven" and this lapse excludes them from the kingdom regardless of their apparent allegiance to Jesus as Lord and exercise of a dynamic ministry in his name (7:21-23). Also, Jesus says that unguarded speech (that is, what people say when they are not trying to dissemble)[26] reveals true character, for "out of the abundance of the heart the mouth speaks" (12:34-37).

The test of character applies to those who teach as well as to those who prophesy. When Jesus tells his followers in 23:8 that they are not to be called "teachers" because they are siblings (*adelphoi*), Matthew's readers are expected to recall Jesus' earlier words in 12:50: "Whoever does the will of my Father in heaven is my brother (*adelphos*) and sister (*adelphē*) and mother." The egalitarian nature of the community that allows for no official teaching office assumes that all members of the community are people who live according to the will of God.

Jesus makes this connection between teaching and obedience to God's will explicit when he says, "Whoever breaks one of the least of these commandments, and teaches others to do the same, will be called least in the kingdom of heaven; but whoever *does them and teaches them* will be called great in the kingdom of heaven" (5:19). The "whoever" of this saying confirms that teaching is potentially the prerogative of any whom God chooses and qualifies, but this openness takes for granted that those who teach the commandments also obey them. As indicated in the excursus on 23:2-7 above, Matthew's Gospel does not allow for any clear distinction between "teaching" and "doing": what one does is part of what one teaches.

The notion that the validity of teaching may be discerned in light of the conduct of the teacher seems foreign in our modern society where teaching is viewed as an objective, academic enterprise. In our world, teachers are respected for being able to present faithfully ideas that they themselves do not endorse or follow. But for Matthew an essential qualification for teaching the commandments of Jesus is an understanding of Jesus' words,

26. For this definition of *pan hrēma argon* in 12:36, see Mark Allan Powell, "Direct and Indirect Phraseology in the Gospel of Matthew," in *SBL 1991 Seminar Papers*, ed. Eugene H. Lovering, Jr. (Atlanta: Scholars Press, 1991), 405–17, esp. 413–16.

and, apparently, Matthew assumes that understanding implies doing. In Matthew, "hear and understand" (13:13-15, 19, 23; 15:10) is virtually synonymous with "hear and do" (7:24, 26; 13:23).[27] Accordingly, if anyone claims to be teaching the commandments of Jesus but is not living in the manner that Jesus said people ought to live, that one's understanding of Jesus' words must be suspect and the teaching of such a one cannot be respected.

Application of this test means that, for Matthew, only those who live according to God's will are to make disciples by teaching the commandments of Jesus. Of course, Matthew knows that people sin (18:7, 15, 21-22), including people who are committed to living in accord with God's will. Jesus' own disciples—the ones to whom the teaching commission is initially given—are persons who, because of cowardice and "little faith," have often failed to do as God wishes. Still, Matthew depicts Jesus' disciples as persons who have made the necessary commitments to the rule of God, sacrificing everything else for its sake (19:27-29; compare 4:20, 22; 9:9). This overall orientation, which Matthew calls "seeking the kingdom" (6:33), seems to be of more importance than the total absence of individual failings. Forgiveness abounds (18:21-27), but the ones who teach obedience to God's will must, for Matthew, be ones who are committed to obeying God's will themselves.

A third test that Matthew's Gospel offers for determining the legitimacy of teaching is the consensus or agreement of the community. Jesus gives to the church at large the authority to "bind and loose" (18:18).[28] According to Matthew, this teaching function may be exercised by any member of the community but, in cases where disputes arise, must be exercised by the church as a whole.

In Matthew 18:15-18, Jesus details how this test is to be applied. He describes a scenario in which one member of the com-

27. This is perhaps most clear in a literal rendering of 13:23. The one who hears (akouō) and understands (suniēmi) is the one who "does" (poieō).

28. As one who is not to be called "rabbi," Peter cannot be envisioned as exercising any supreme or exclusive rabbinic function within the community. As 18:15-18 makes clear, the authority given to Peter in 16:19 is given to him as a representative of the church that Jesus will build. See Jack Dean Kingsbury, "The Figure of Peter in Matthew's Gospel as a Theological Problem," JBL 98 (1979): 67–83; and Michael J. Wilkins, The Concept of Disciple in Matthew's Gospel (NovTSup 59; Leiden: E. J. Brill, 1988), 173–216.

munity goes to another in private in order to tell him that he is sinning. By designating the sinful person as a "brother," Jesus indicates that he is a member of a community in which all are regarded as equals (23:8) and that he is a person who normally does the will of God (12:50). The implication, then, is that this person is transgressing God's will unwittingly. Thus, the one who comes to him is envisioned as exercising a teaching function within the community. When the sinful brother refuses to listen, furthermore, the implication is not that he wishes stubbornly to persist in sin but that he refuses to accept the opinion that his conduct is a violation of God's will. The process, then, is to seek the counsel of two or three other community members and, ultimately, to bring the dispute to the whole church. If he refuses to listen even to the church, then the community may no longer regard him as a brother. Now he is to them "as a Gentile or a tax collector," that is, as an outsider whose fellowship they desire but who must be taught to obey the commandments of Jesus before he can be regarded as one who has been made a disciple.[29]

For Matthew, the person who is committed to living according to the will of God but who disagrees with other community members concerning what sort of conduct is sinful must allow the church as a whole to exercise its preeminent teaching function of binding and loosing to settle the dispute.[30] Although any individual member of the church may teach the commandments

29. Whatever its original meaning, the phrase "Gentiles and tax collectors" no longer denotes those who are to be despised and rejected. In this narrative, Jesus calls tax collectors (9:9-13; see also 11:19; 21:32) and his disciples go to Gentiles (28:19) so that Gentiles and tax collectors may become part of the community.
30. Many scholars who recognize that "binding and loosing" refers to determination of what is allowed or forbidden in Matt 16:19 think the phrase has acquired a different sense in 18:18, namely, that of expelling from and admitting to the community. See David L. Bartlett, *Ministry in the New Testament* (OBT; Minneapolis: Fortress Press, 1993), 71-76; Beare, 355-56, 380; Meier, *Vision*, 113-14, 132; and Eduard Schweizer, *The Good News according to Matthew*, trans. David E. Green (Atlanta: John Knox Press, 1975), 371-72. But the proposal that Matthew uses these technical terms in two different ways is as unnecessary as it is unlikely. The references to binding and loosing in 18:18 do not refer to excommunication procedures per se but to the determination of acceptable conduct that will form the basis for decisions regarding expulsion and admission. Both 16:19 and 18:18 envision the binding and loosing of laws, not of people, although as 18:18 makes clear, determination of the extent to which cer-

of Jesus, every individual member must respect the view of the whole church when it reaches agreement.[31]

CONCLUSION: THE GOAL OF TEACHING

The goal of the teaching ministry of the church according to Matthew is to make disciples (28:18-20). A disciple is a member of Jesus' family who does the will of God (12:50). In the Sermon on the Mount, Matthew presents the goal of Jesus' own teaching ministry as being to produce people who "do the will of the Father" (7:21-27), who are "perfect, even as the heavenly Father is perfect" (5:48). To be "perfect" (*teleios*) means to live in complete accord with God's will, to be a person whose actions (5:23, 38-42), words (5:22, 33-37), thoughts (5:28), attitudes (5:43-44), and motives (6:1-6, 16-18) are pleasing to God.

Elsewhere, Matthew records Jesus as saying that, while a disciple is not above his teacher, "it is enough for the disciple to be like the teacher" (10:24-25a). Since Jesus himself is the one true teacher of all disciples (23:8, 10), we may also define the goal of teaching as being to make disciples who are "like Jesus." Clearly, to be like Jesus does not mean to entertain messianic aspirations (24:5, 24) or to assume the sort of authority reserved for him alone (23:8-10). Rather, disciples of Jesus are to become like their teacher with regard to the matter that is the subject of his teaching, ethical obedience to the will of God. They are to live in accord with God's will as surely as Jesus did, knowing full well that they will be maligned for doing so (10:25b).

In short, Matthew presents the goal of the church's teaching ministry as being to form baptized members of the community into disciples who, like Jesus, live in perfect accord with God's will. Whether this goal is existentially attainable does not interest Matthew in the least. The goal remains a worthy one regardless, such that any member of the community who is not yet living in accord with God's will as perfectly as Jesus did still needs to benefit from the teaching ministry of the church.

---

tain laws are binding for the community inevitably affects determination of membership in the community.

31. The seemingly obvious question of what to do if the church cannot reach agreement is not considered by Matthew.

CHAPTER FOUR

STEWARDSHIP

In pastoral theology today stewardship comprises a wide variety of concerns, different aspects of which may be considered by committees devoted to budget planning, seminars focusing on time management, or task forces committed to ecological responsibility.[1] At base, however, concepts of stewardship are almost always informed by three parables of Jesus, all of which are found in the Gospel of Matthew (21:33-43; 24:45-51; 25:14-30).[2] Curiously, the actual word for "steward" (*oikonomos*) is not used in these parables or anywhere else in Matthew's Gospel.[3] In a strict sense, a steward (*oikonomos*) was a person who managed a household at the discretion of a "householder" (*oikodespotēs*).[4] Something analogous to this is assumed in the Matthean parables

---

1. For a helpful study of biblical and historical understandings of stewardship, see John Reumann, *Stewardship and the Economy of God* (Grand Rapids: Wm. B. Eerdmans, 1992).

2. For discussion and bibliography on these parables, see the usual commentaries on Matthew and see also John R. Donahue, *The Gospel in Parable* (Philadelphia: Fortress Press, 1988), 63–105; John Drury, *The Parables in the Gospels* (New York: Crossroad, 1985), 70–107; Jan Lambrecht, *Out of the Treasure: The Parables in the Gospel of Matthew* (LTPM 10; Louvain: Peeters Press, 1991), 105–25, 183–98, 217–44; and Bernard Brandon Scott, *Hear Then the Parable: A Commentary on the Parables of Jesus* (Minneapolis: Fortress Press, 1989), 205–13, 217–54.

3. Luke's Gospel is the only one that uses *oikonomos*, at 12:42 (par Matt 24:45) and at 16:1, 3, 8. Similarly, the Greek words for "stewardship" (*oikonomia*) and "to be a steward" (*oikonomeō*) do not occur in the Gospels outside of Luke 16:2-4. The term *epitropos* (Matt 20:18) is sometimes translated "steward" in English Bibles but actually refers to a "supervisor," to a person in charge of hiring and assigning work to other workers.

4. Householders are mentioned in Matthew's Gospel at 10:25; 13:27, 52; 20:1, 11; 21:33; 24:43. On Matthew's understanding of the church as a house-

where God is portrayed allegorically as a lord (*kyrios*) who allows tenants (*georgous*) or servants (*doulous*) to manage his property and possessions.

Taking our cue from these parables and moving on to consider the whole of Matthew's Gospel, we will describe what Matthew considers to be the theological basis for stewardship, the primary incentive for stewards to be faithful, and the principles that determine whether stewardship is faithful or not. We will illustrate our findings with regard to stewardship of human relationships and stewardship of material possessions.

BASIS

Christian theologians have sought to define the basis for stewardship with reference to a number of biblical doctrines. T. A. Kantonen speaks broadly of stewardship that may be related to creation, to redemption, and to sanctification.[5] Douglas John Hall interprets Jesus' stewardship parables in light of the Old Testament doctrine of election.[6] John Reumann discusses the "economy of God," a concept that encompasses salvation history, creation theology, and apocalyptic eschatology.[7] When we narrow our discussion to focus on Matthew's Gospel, however, we find that the concept of stewardship here derives from what may be this Gospel's principal theme—its doctrine of the reign of God. The notion that God's people are stewards entrusted with the care of God's domain is a corollary to the belief that God is "Lord of heaven and earth" (11:25; see also 5:34-35) and that all things therefore belong to God.

This understanding is evident in the three stewardship parables (21:33-43; 24:45-51; 25:14-30). In every case, the people depicted in these parables are permitted to use what does not actually belong to them. The master's generosity imposes responsibility as well as privilege: servants are held accountable for how

hold, see Michael H. Crosby, *House of Disciples: Church, Economics, and Justice in Matthew* (Maryknoll, N.Y.: Orbis Books, 1988).

    5. T. A. Kantonen, "The Scriptural and Theological Basis for Evangelism and Stewardship," *LQ* 3 (1951): 271–77.

    6. Douglas John Hall, *The Steward: A Biblical Symbol Come of Age* (New York: Friendship Press, 1985), 19–20.

    7. Reumann, *Stewardship*, 77–113.

they use what belongs to their lord. These parables make the point that all we have (or apparently have) actually belongs to God. But they will prove misleading if we press the allegorical elements too far. In real life, the lords depicted in the parables would suffer severe losses if their servants did not give them the fruit of the harvest (21:33-37), mismanaged their household (24:48-49), or failed to invest their money (25:26-27). The God of Matthew's Gospel, however, is not dependent on human beings. A God who can create children of Abraham from stones (3:9) does not really have to worry about whether servants are being good stewards or not. The integrity of God's reign is secure nevertheless.

In fact, the reverse is true. If God is not dependent on humans for anything, humans are dependent on God for everything. The God of Matthew's Gospel provides for human needs, sending rain on the righteous and the unrighteous and making the sun to shine on the good and bad alike (5:45). God knows what people need even before they ask (6:8) and so gives daily bread (6:11), providing food and clothing with the same care evident in the world of nature (6:26-32). And since people cannot live on bread alone (4:4), since life is more than food and the body more than clothing (6:25), God also provides for more transcendent human needs. The word of God offers the way of life (6:14; see also 4:4), and the mercy of God offers forgiveness of sins (6:14; 12:31). As another parable shows, we are not only servants of God but debtors (18:23-34).

In brief, the theological basis for stewardship in Matthew's Gospel may be stated as follows: *We ourselves and everything that we apparently possess actually belong to God, on whom we are dependent for everything and to whom we owe a debt that we can never repay.* We may note that such a basis lacks any specifically Christian content. Paul, by contrast, links the awareness that we are not our own to Christ's redemptive sacrifice: we have been "bought with a price" (1 Cor 6:19-20). Although Matthew's Gospel can speak of Jesus' death as a ransom (20:28), the ethical corollary it offers to this point is not that we therefore belong to God but that we ought to follow Christ's example in serving one another (20:25-28). That we belong to God is a point Matthew regards as already established, implicit in the identification of God as Lord of heaven and earth.

Thus, Matthew's understanding of the theological basis for stewardship is pre-Christian, rooted in a truth to which Jesus testifies but which he does not need to establish. Still, the announcement that the reign of God has now come near (3:2; 4:17; 10:7) and is specifically present in the work of Jesus (12:28) expedites evaluation of one's stewardship. For Matthew's readers, the call to be good stewards is included in this Gospel's summons to repentance (3:2; 4:17). In addition, Matthew's understanding of the church as the eschatological community of Christ (16:18-19; 18:18-20) shifts the focus for stewardship within that community "from management to mission."[8]

MOTIVE

The primary motive for responsible stewardship in the Gospel of Matthew derives from the theological basis articulated above. Awareness that all things come from God is expected to inspire *gratitude*. The wise and faithful steward (24:45) does not resent being dependent on God but, rather, appreciates the divine providence and generosity that begets such dependence.

In an idealized sense, gratitude may be expressed as joy. The Magi are moved by their great joy at finding the Christ child to offer him treasures (2:10-11). Likewise, discovery of God's kingdom may inspire joy so great that one will give up everything to obtain it (13:44). Conversely, one who chooses earthly riches over treasure in heaven does so not with joy but with sorrow (19:22). Ultimately, however, Matthew is distrustful of joy as a basis for discipleship (13:20-21), and so this Gospel prefers to present faithful stewardship as a response of duty. This, too, is an expression of gratitude. The grateful person becomes committed to a way of living that is to be followed without regard for emotional disposition.

The notion that duty (as an expression of gratitude) may serve as a suitable motive for stewardship is augmented on a practical level with incentives that derive from this Gospel's theology of

8. I derive this alliterative phrase from the unpublished teaching of Dennis A. Anderson.

recompense.[9] Good stewards will be generously rewarded and bad stewards will be severely punished. While such appeals are not incompatible with the basic motive of gratitude, they may seem unnecessary. Ideally, grateful stewards will live according to the principles articulated in this Gospel out of a sense of duty rather than simply to earn rewards and avoid punishments. But Matthew is realistic regarding the failures of those with good motives (26:41). In any case, the incentives of recompense warrant our attention if only because they are explicitly linked with stewardship repeatedly throughout this book.

The theme is stressed in each of the three stewardship parables. In one, the lord will put the unworthy tenants "to a miserable death, and lease the vineyard to other tenants who will give him the produce at the harvest time" (21:41). In another, the master will place the faithful servant "in charge of all his possessions" (24:47) but will cut the unfaithful servant in pieces and "put him with the hypocrites, where there will be weeping and gnashing of teeth" (24:51). And in the third, the master puts his trustworthy servants in charge of many things, inviting them to "enter into the joy" of their master (25:21, 23), while the unworthy servant is stripped of what little he has and is thrown into the outer darkness where, again, "there will be weeping and gnashing of teeth" (25:28-30).

The apocalyptic tone of these parables implies that recompense for faithful and unfaithful stewardship is received at the end of time, when the Lord comes (21:40; 24:46, 50; 25:19). In general, all references to punishment in Matthew appear to be linked to the final judgment, and this Gospel displays concern that none be punished prematurely (8:29-32; 13:28-30). References to reward are more ambiguous but probably should also be read in this light. For example, the rewards that are promised for practicing piety in secret (6:1-6, 16-18) may be illustrative of the "treasures in heaven" that Jesus' disciples are encouraged to accumulate (6:20; see also 19:21). Notably, in 19:27-30, Jesus

9. Scholars have long noted that Matthew gives more extensive treatment to the themes of reward and punishment than the other Synoptics. See Blaine Charette, *The Theme of Recompense in Matthew's Gospel* (JSNTSS 79; Sheffield: JSOT Press, 1992); Daniel Marquerat, *Le jugement dans l'évangile de Matthieu* (Geneva: Labor et Fides, 1981).

promises his followers future blessings only, whereas the parallel passages in Mark and Luke speak also of benefits received now "in this time" (Mark 10:30, Luke 18:30). Or, again, since Matthew knows that those who are righteous may be maligned in this life (5:10-11; 10:25), passages such as 7:2b ("The measure you give will be the measure you get") must be understood as referring to the future, when the Son of Man will "repay everyone" for what they have done (16:27; see also 7:2a). Thus, although Matthew's Gospel does not rule out the possibility of God rewarding (or punishing) people in this life, what it says of recompense is certainly future-oriented.

Temporal disjuncture, however, is not expected to diminish the effectiveness of recompense as an incentive for responsible stewardship (or for discipleship in general). Anticipation of a future reward brings joy already in the present, even for those who are suffering (5:12). A wait may be involved, but the reward, when it comes, will be eternal (19:29; 25:46). Good stewards may be assured that the treasure that awaits them is incorruptible (6:20) and that any losses they may suffer now will be repaid a hundredfold (19:29). Of course, punishment is eternal also (25:46; see also 18:8; 25:41).

Matthew's theology of recompense is more developed with regard to reward than punishment, and this is significant for the use of recompense as a motivating factor for stewardship within the community. Although Matthew's Gospel knows no degrees of punishment, it does speak of stratification within the kingdom of heaven according to which the position of some may be greater or lesser than others (5:19; 18:4). While admission to the kingdom of heaven is the basic reward for the righteous (13:43; 25:46), the practice of good stewardship allows those who will gain entrance to "store up treasures" there (6:20), that is, to increase the greatness of their reward in proportion to their faithfulness (10:41). This perspective reduces the link between stewardship and soteriology and allows the theology of recompense to continue to function as a motivating factor for those who already count themselves among the saved. While stewards may prove to be so unfaithful that the kingdom of God must be taken away from them (21:43), faithful stewardship is more often presented as a means of accruing benefits within the kingdom than as a way of securing admission to the kingdom itself.

PRINCIPLES

Numerous passages in Matthew's Gospel are informed by the notion that people are stewards of God and ought to live their lives in recognition of all that this implies. We may summarize this Gospel's idea of what constitutes good stewardship in terms of three principles:

1. Good stewards have only one master (6:24). Matthew's Gospel cites the Hebrew scriptures to affirm that people should worship and serve the Lord God only (4:10; see Deut 6:13) and love the Lord God with all the heart, soul, and mind (22:37; see Deut 6:5). Allegiance to anything that competes with our devotion to God as our one master must be tempered or renounced. As such, this principle is traditional for Judaism, but it is developed in Matthew's Gospel through transference of God's unique prerogatives to Jesus. The unique status of Jesus as Son of God (11:27) allows for a certain blurring of identities between God and Jesus, as may be observed in the baptismal formula where "Father, Son, and Holy Spirit" is regarded as a single name (28:19). Thus, as we observed in chapter 2 above, worship of Jesus may be commended without violating the mandate that worship is for God alone (4:10; compare 2:11; 8:2; 9:18; 14:33; 15:25; 20:20; 28:9, 17). Similarly, the one to whom we are to show exclusive devotion may be identified, interchangeably, as "the Father" (23:9) or "the Christ" (23:10). The relationship of stewards to God as "Lord of heaven and earth" (11:25) does not differ in any practical sense from their relationship to Jesus as the one to whom "all authority in heaven and on earth" has been given (28:18).

Matthew's Gospel emphasizes the precedence of Jesus over respected persons and cherished institutions. Jesus is mightier than John the Baptist (3:11, 14) and greater than Jonah or Solomon (12:41-42). He is David's lord (22:41-46), and his teaching supersedes that of Moses (19:8-9). He is greater than the temple (12:6) and "lord of the sabbath" (12:8). From these references we may infer that having one master necessitates prioritization of all commitments, including those that are commendable in and of themselves. Good stewardship means more than just worshiping the Lord rather than Satan (4:8-10) or serving God rather than mammon (6:24). Good stewardship means keeping our allegiance to the one master so absolute that even worthy concerns remain subordinate.

2. Good stewards acknowledge their master in word and deed (10:32-33). Matthew's Gospel permits no secret discipleship. Those who have one master ought to make this known by living in ways that acknowledge the relationship. Matthew's Gospel, then, is fundamentally concerned with stewardship of *life*, especially as life is expressed through words and deeds.

Acknowledging Christ through word includes making public one's commitment to him. In 10:32-33, Matthew contrasts acknowledging Christ before people with denying Christ before people. The latter is illustrated in the Gospel when Peter insists that he is not "with Jesus" and swears, "I do not know the man!" (26:69-75). Acknowledging Christ as our master, then, may mean doing the opposite of what Peter does; it may mean affirming publicly that we belong to Christ even when it is inconvenient or dangerous for us to do so.

But to acknowledge Christ through words has a broader application than explicit public witness. It means also that our words ought to be appropriate for one who is a servant of Christ. According to Matthew's Gospel, speech reveals what is in the heart. Obviously, people can dissemble and say things that they do not really mean (22:15-18), but in general, the mouth speaks "out of the abundance of the heart" (12:34). What comes out of the mouth is what defiles a person because it "proceeds from the heart" (15:18). Matthew's Gospel gives no credence to the notion that what one *does* rather than what one *says* is what counts.[10] Instead, this Gospel affirms that "by your words you will be justified, and by your words you will be condemned" (12:37). Thus, people who wish to acknowledge Christ as their master will not speak insults (5:22), swear oaths (5:34), offer pretentious prayers (6:5), pronounce judgment (7:2), or in other ways disavow their allegiance to Jesus through words that are unworthy of him.

Acknowledging Christ through deeds means carrying out in action the commitments that one makes verbally. Words alone are not enough, for to call Jesus "Lord" is ultimately meaningless

10. On Matt 23:2-3, see the discussion above, pp. 75–81.

if one does not do what he wants, namely, to obey the will of his
Father (7:21). This point is best illustrated in the parable of the
Two Sons (21:28-31), which presents actual performance of a
deed as the bottom-line determination of obedience. The son
who promises to work in the vineyard but does not fails to do the
will of his father. In light of what was said above, the point of the
parable cannot be that deeds reveal one's true devotion better
than words. Rather, since words do reveal what is in the heart,
empty promises demonstrate a lack of true devotion. In order for
our words not to be in vain and revelatory of a heart far from
God (15:8-9), they must be accompanied by actions that corre-
spond to the will of our master.

3. *Good stewards prove themselves worthy of their master's trust.*
Each of the three stewardship parables in Matthew's Gospel describes a scenario in which people are entrusted with specific responsibilities and held accountable to their master for the
manner in which these are fulfilled. Taken together, the parables
provide three examples of how stewards may fail. In the most
crass instance, the stewards rebel against their master and attempt to keep for themselves what should be given to him
(21:33-39). In another case, the steward simply grows lax and be-
haves as though he will never have to give account for his actions
(24:45-51). And in the third instance, the steward fears the
master so greatly that he does nothing at all (25:24-25). Notably,
the stewards in these three instances are condemned and punished equally, regardless of whether their failure is motivated by
rebellion, sloth, or fear (21:40-41; 24:51; 25:30). Stewards who
fail to fulfill the expectations of their master are "wicked" (21:41;
24:48), "evil" (25:26), "lazy" (25:26), and "worthless" (25:30).
Those who do fulfill their master's expectations are "good"
(25:21, 23), "faithful" (24:45; 25:21, 23), and "wise" (24:45).

This third principle of stewardship is derivative of the second
insofar as acknowledging the master in word and deed obviously
implies fulfillment of the master's trust. The problems of the
stewards in the first two parables may be viewed as failures to acknowledge their master in the very areas where responsibility has
been entrusted to them. In the third parable, however, this failure
is more subtle. Here, the servant is careful not to lose or misman-
age that which he knows is not his. When he returns the master's

property undamaged (but also unused), he can say, "Here, you have what is yours" (25:25). He does acknowledge his master's claim, but this response is still not acceptable. According to Matthew's Gospel, acknowledgment that what we apparently possess actually belongs to God is an important part of stewardship, but even this is not the sum of the matter. Faithful stewardship also demands that we use what has been entrusted to us and that we do so in a responsible manner.

These three principles of stewardship may apply in many domains of life, but we will illustrate them with respect to two areas that receive special attention in Matthew's Gospel: human relationships and material possessions.

HUMAN RELATIONSHIPS

Although Matthew's Gospel has a strong communal focus that affirms the importance of human relationships, it also warns that such relationships may compromise our commitment to God. Several times this Gospel indicates that we ought to be more concerned with what God thinks of us than with the opinions of humans. This is why works of piety ought to be done in secret (6:1-6, 16-18), and it is why we should not fear those who can kill the body but not the soul (10:28). At its most extreme, this perspective presents the ways of God and the ways of humans as irreconcilably opposed to each other. Jesus' rebuke to Peter in 16:23 is particularly telling: "Get behind me, Satan! . . . You are setting your mind not on divine things but on human things." This verse would seem to place humans and Satan on one side of a dichotomy and God on the other.

As we shall see, the matter is more complex for Matthew than these initial observations suggest. Still, the Gospel's first stewardship principle prohibits any human relationship from interfering with our absolute commitment to God (or Jesus) as our one master. This is especially true with regard to our closest and most intimate relationships, those within our own families. Jesus insists, "Whoever loves father or mother more than me is not worthy of me; and whoever loves son or daughter more than me is not worthy of me" (10:37). Jesus is presented, furthermore, as fully cognizant of the radical consequences his demand could have: "I have not come to bring peace, but a sword. For I have come to set a man against his father, and a daughter against her mother, and a daughter-in-law against her mother-in-law; and one's foes will be members of one's own household" (10:34-36; see also Mic 7:6).

Renunciation of relationships, then, may be necessary to preserve the integrity of our commitment to Christ. A subtle example of such renunciation may be found in the call of James and John when Matthew notes that in response to Jesus' summons the two brothers "left the boat *and their father*, and followed him" (4:22). A less subtle example is seen in the case of the unnamed disciple who wishes to bury his father before following Jesus but is told, "Follow me, and let the dead bury their own dead" (8:22).

We have indicated that Matthew's Gospel draws on a theology of recompense to provide incentive for what it regards as good stewardship. This is explicitly the case with human relationships. In recognition that renunciation of such relationships may be especially hard, this Gospel offers Jesus' promise that those who leave "brothers or sisters or father or mother or children" for his sake will receive a hundredfold in the new world (19:28-29). A foretaste of this future reward may be experienced even now in the community of Jesus' followers, for Jesus claims that "whoever does the will of my Father in heaven is my brother and sister and mother" (12:50). The words used here, however, reflect a concern that even the relationships within this community be subordinate. The terms "brother and sister and mother" liken Jesus' followers only to those family members who are not perceived as authority figures in the patriarchal world of Matthew's story. No one in the community is to be called "father," Jesus says, because such status is reserved for God alone (23:9). Likewise, there are to be no hierarchical offices for teaching, because Christ is the one teacher (23:8, 10).

Thus, Matthew's Gospel betrays the same concern with regard to relationships within the community of faith that it does for family relationships, namely, a concern that commitments to other human beings not be allowed to infringe on exclusive devotion to God or Jesus. Matthew's first stewardship principle requires not only restriction of negative orientations, such as fear of humans or desire for glory, but also restriction of positive ones, such as devotion to family and respect for community leaders. This is what it means to have one master (6:24).

Matthew's second stewardship principle goes a step farther. In addition to prioritizing human relationships so that they do not challenge God's role as our one master, we are to acknowledge God as master of those relationships. The relationships are not really "ours" at all. According to Matthew's Gospel, God gives people to each other, places them in relationship with each other, and holds them accountable for their conduct within these relationships. We do not *have* relationships with others; we are stewards of relationships that are given to us by God.

This point is illustrated most poignantly in Matthew's Gospel with reference to divorce (5:31-32; 19:3-9). The strong disapproval of divorce that we find in this Gospel may be based on many factors, including a concern for justice to women, who were invariably placed at a disadvantage.[11] But Matthew also presents divorce as a stewardship issue. The person who divorces his wife errs in thinking that this relationship is his to end. It makes no difference that Moses allowed certificates of divorce to be written, and presumably it would make no difference if the wife wanted to end the relationship also. The point for Matthew is that *no one*—not the husband, not the wife, not even Moses—has the authority to separate those whom God has joined together (19:6b). From Matthew's perspective, seeking a divorce for any reason other than *porneia* (unchastity? unlawful union?)[12] represents a failure to acknowledge God as master of our relationships. Insistence on such acknowledgment is what costs John the Baptist his life (14:3-4).

The sentiment against divorce is so strong in Matthew's Gospel that it colors what is said about human relationships in general. We observed earlier that Matthew commends renunciation of relationships that prevent us from making a total commitment to God or to Jesus. But though the Gospel speaks of people

11. Phillip Segal, *The Halakah of Jesus of Nazareth according to the Gospel of Matthew* (New York: University Press of America, 1986), 94, 116.

12. For a summary of the discussion on various interpretations given to the exception that Matthew makes for *porneia*, see Raymond F. Collins, *Divorce in the New Testament* (GNS 38; Collegeville, Minn.: Liturgical Press, 1992), 184–213.

leaving their brothers, sisters, father, mother, and children for Jesus' sake (19:29; see also 10:34-37), it does not mention people leaving their spouses. We know from Paul's epistles that commitments to Jesus sometimes did lead to marital separation (1 Cor 7:12-16), but this is a problem that Matthew's Gospel manages not to address. We may sense, then, the potential for tension between Matthew's first and second stewardship principles as they apply to human relationships. The Gospel calls us, on the one hand, to renounce relationships that challenge God's reign as our Lord and, on the other, to preserve relationships in deference to that reign. The two points are not necessarily contradictory, for ideally all relationships might be preserved in subordination to God's rule. Yet in a less than ideal world, one can imagine any number of scenarios (including that addressed by Paul in 1 Corinthians 7) where the principles could conflict.

This potential increases when we look at Matthew's third principle. If human relationships are given to us by God, then we ought to view them as a trust from God for which we will be held accountable. Such accountability extends to all our relationships in ways analogous to what has been said of marriage. Specifically, Matthew emphasizes accountability for relationships with one's immediate family and with other members of the community of faith, the same two areas that received emphasis in discussion of the first principle above. With regard to immediate family, stewards are expected to value children (18:4-5, 10; 19:13-15), honor their parents (15:3-9), and live peaceably with their siblings (5:22-24). With regard to other members of the community, stewards are to serve one another (20:26-27), forgive one another (6:12, 14-15; 18:21-35), and seek always to preserve (18:15-20) and restore (5:23-24; 18:12-14) relationships.[13]

How are we to reconcile the charge to honor father and mother (15:3-9) with the commendations for leaving father and mother for Jesus' sake (19:29)? Or, for that matter, how are we to reconcile the expectation that we will be servants of other community members (20:26-27) with the demand that we serve no

---

13. Since familial terms are often used metaphorically in Matthew (12:50), we should not restrict interpretation of passages using these terms to a single reading. Passages such as 5:22-24 may refer to blood relatives, to community members, or to both.

one but God (4:10; 6:24)? At first, we might assume that the point is simply prioritization: we do well to honor our parents or serve one another as long as we put God or Jesus *first*. This does seem to be the point of Jesus' complaint against those who love others *more than* him in 10:37. But we cannot always adjudicate the tensions between Matthew's stewardship principles by giving priority to the devotion shown most obviously to God or Jesus. If we did, we would have to grant the appropriateness of giving as a religious offering what might have been spent providing for our parents. And we would expect the presentation of a gift to God to take precedence over making peace with another human being. Yet in cases such as these, Matthew's Gospel appears to overturn the idea that devotion shown to God or to Jesus is more important than that shown to other human beings (15:3-9; 5:23-24).

A clue to resolving this puzzle may be found in Matthew's account of the Great Commandments (22:34-40). Jesus does not present the second commandment ("Love your neighbor as yourself") as subordinate to the first ("Love the Lord your God"). Rather, he says the second is *like* the first (22:39). Far from being antithetical or even competitive, devotion to God and neighbor are here defined as virtually synonymous. Serving God implies obedience to God's will, and, according to Matthew's Gospel, God's will is that we love our neighbors (and enemies) and serve one another. Thus, the paradox: we are to serve only God, but since God tells us to serve others, we cannot fulfill the command to serve only God except by serving others.

This paradox is grounded in two theological presuppositions concerning the nature of God's reign. First, we serve a master who does not need servants. As we have seen, the very basis for stewardship in Matthew's Gospel is the assumption that God is Lord of heaven and earth, and this implies that God is not dependent on us for anything. If this is true, then, in a practical sense, the only way we can effectively serve God is through service to others. Second, we serve a master who is devoted to serving us. Jesus says, "The Son of Man came not to be served but to serve" (20:28). From Matthew's perspective, our service to God is reflective of God's own prior commitment to humanity. God has determined that our obligations to God should be fulfilled in interactions with each other. We see this in the numerous sayings of Jesus that identify what we do for others as being truly done for him (10:40; 18:5; 25:35-40, 42-45). We see it also in the sayings on forgiveness that allow us to forgive the debts of others in lieu of paying our own debts to God (6:12, 14-15; 18:23-35).

Matthew's Gospel offers principles for stewardship rather than clear-cut directives, but within the full scheme of Matthew's theology the tensions inherent in these principles can be resolved in ways that are fairly consistent. To illustrate, let us consider further two specific instances mentioned above.

First, in 26:6-13, Jesus commends a woman for anointing him with ointment that his disciples say could have been "sold for a large sum, and the money given to the poor." Here, the tension seems to be resolved in favor of the principle that devotion to Jesus is to have an exclusive priority uncompromised even by commitments that are otherwise commendable. But the concern for showing responsible stewardship through service to other human beings (in this case, the poor) is not slighted here. Jesus says, "You always have the poor with you, but you will not always have me." The second part of this verse (26:11b) must be compared to what Jesus says in 28:20b at the conclusion of the Gospel: "I am with you always, to the end of the age." Matthew's readers must realize that in some sense they *will* always have Jesus with them, but not in the same sense in which he was present with his disciples in Bethany (see also 9:15). In what sense will he be with them always? At least a partial answer to this question is supplied elsewhere in this Gospel: he will be present in the poor, the needy, and the helpless, such that what is done for them is truly done for him (10:40; 18:5; 25:35-40, 42-45).

Far from creating a dichotomy between love for Jesus and service to the poor, this passage suggests that service to the poor is an alternative means of demonstrating the sort of devotion to Jesus evidenced by the woman in the story. Jesus' comment that "you always have the poor with you" indicates that selling the ointment and giving the money to the poor would indeed be a good idea if he were not now overtly present in a way that he will not be later. For Matthew's readers, then, giving to the poor becomes an indirect means of showing devotion to Jesus in those days when the type of devotion shown to him by the woman in this story is no longer an option. In short, Jesus agrees with his disciples that selling one's possessions and giving to the poor is a good thing (see 19:21). What he objects to is their presentation of this as something that one does *instead of* showing devotion to Jesus. For Matthew's Gospel, the motivation behind ostensibly good actions is always important (6:1-6, 16-18). One ought to give to the poor as an expression of one's devotion to God rather than as an expression of devotion to a competing concern.

Second, in 5:23-24, Jesus affirms that seeking reconciliation with a sibling is to take precedence over offering a gift to God at the altar. Here, the tension between Matthew's stewardship principles appears to be resolved in favor of responsible preservation of the relationships God has entrusted to us. But the principle of making exclusive devotion to God our highest priority is not really compromised here. Elsewhere, Matthew's Gospel affirms that God prefers mercy to sacrifice (9:13; 12:7; compare Hos 6:6). The person who is about to offer God a sacrifice but then goes instead to mend a broken relationship offers God a better gift than what was originally intended. Such a one does not choose to place human relationships over relationship with God; rather, the person demonstrates devotion to God in the way that God prefers to see such devotion expressed.

MATERIAL POSSESSIONS

The very concept of possessions is ironic according to Matthew's understanding of stewardship, although Matthew's Gospel does use the everyday language of ownership with which we are all accustomed. A man can be said to *buy* a field or a pearl (13:44-46), and if he has a hundred sheep, then they *belong* to him (18:12). People can *sell* their possessions (*hyparchonta*, 19:21; *ktēma*, 19:22) or have their property (*skeuē*) *stolen* from them (12:29; see also 6:19). Such language recognizes that control of material items is to be exercised by those whom society sanctions according to its codes of ownership. Still, in Matthew's view, such ownership is ultimately illusory, transcended by the recognition that all things belong to God. As the Son of God, Jesus does not need to worry about such petty concerns. If he needs animals for his ride into Jerusalem, he can simply send for them. And if anyone objects, his answer will be, "The Lord needs them." Good stewards will know what this means (21:2-3).

Matthew's Gospel articulates its theology of recompense with specific reference to stewardship of material possessions, just as it

did with regard to human relationships. This Gospel promises
that those who give up such material things as lands or houses for
Jesus' sake will be repaid a hundredfold and will inherit eternal
life (19:29). Likewise, those who give even a cup of cold water to
one of Jesus' disciples will be rewarded (10:42). Those who provide lodging for missionaries will be blessed with peace (10:11-
13), and those who care for even the least of Jesus' family will
inherit the kingdom (10:34; 25:34-40). By contrast, those who
will not give up their possessions will not enter the kingdom of
heaven (19:21-24), and those who refuse to provide for Jesus' followers will meet with a harsh judgment (10:15) and suffer eternal
punishment (25:46).

With this in mind, let us apply Matthew's principles of stewardship to a consideration of material possessions and see how
they work out in practice. The first principle, that a good steward
serves only one master, is established in Matthew with specific
reference to material possessions: "You cannot serve God and
mammon"[14] (6:24). People who are truly serving God and not
mammon are able to give up their material possessions. Jesus'
disciples serve as good examples of stewardship in this regard, for
they leave everything to follow him (4:20, 22; 19:27). The rich
young man who turns away sorrowful when Jesus tells him to
give up his possessions is a tragic example of a slave to mammon
(19:21-22; compare 6:24). The call to give up everything is also
echoed in Jesus' parable of the treasure in the field (13:44) and of
the great pearl (13:45-46). Both stories describe the reign of God
as a discovery so great that people will gladly give up all they have
in order to obtain it.

When Matthew presents Jesus as sending his disciples out in
mission, the severity of their austere lifestyle is emphasized.
They are to remain dependent on others for such basic needs as
food and lodging (10:10-11). They are to do without sandals,
staffs, bags, spare tunics, and money in their belts (10:9-10). Furthermore, Matthew's Gospel differs from both Mark and Luke in
that it does not describe this mission as being completed within

14. Here I retain the translation of *mamōna* used in KJV and RSV because
the NRSV reading "wealth" is too limited. Immediate context indicates that
serving mammon does not just mean "delight in riches" (13:22) but also concern for such basic necessities as food and clothing (6:25).

the time period covered by the story (see Mark 6:30; Luke 9:10; 10:17). Thus, the requirements presented here are not temporally conditioned, and their applicability to Matthew's readers is enhanced. Since in Matthew, Jesus insists that this mission will continue until the parousia (10:23), Matthew's readers are clearly expected to believe that there will still be followers of Jesus in their day who abandon virtually all of their possessions to become missionaries.

Other passages in Matthew suggest that divestment of possessions is an expectation even for those who are not engaged in specialized ministries. The demand that Jesus makes of the rich young man in 19:21-22 should be considered normative rather than exceptional because it is explicitly connected to two commands of Jesus that all who wish to become disciples must be taught to obey (28:19-20). Jesus has previously declared that his followers must "be perfect" (5:48), and he has exhorted them to "store up treasures in heaven" (6:20). Now, he tells the rich young man, "If you wish to *be perfect*, go, sell your possessions, and give the money to the poor, and you will have *treasure in heaven*." Thus, even readers who are not called to be missionaries are expected to realize that divestment of possessions is part of basic discipleship, required for obedience to generic commands.

The demand for divestment that Matthew presents as normative for all stewards differs from that articulated for missionaries only in degree. Jesus does not tell the rich young man to sell *all* his possessions (19:21; compare Luke 18:22), and Matthew's readers should not assume that a complete divestment of everything they own is necessary to gain treasure in heaven. In the Sermon on the Mount, storing up treasures in heaven is presented as antithetical to storing up treasures on earth (6:19-20). Since Jesus also instructs people in this same sermon to pray for *daily* bread (6:11)[15] and to take no thought for tomorrow (6:34), "storing up treasures on earth" should be taken to mean accumulating more than is required to meet one's basic and immediate needs. Accordingly, people who have accumulated more than they need must now get rid of the surplus if they wish to gain

15. The exact meaning of *epiousios* (usually translated "daily") cannot be determined, but the use of *sēmeron* ("today") in Matthew 6:11 indicates that the petition is for provision of immediate needs.

treasure in heaven. The point is not to make all followers of Jesus dependent on others for charity but to assure that no follower of Jesus has more than he or she needs. In some cases, the divestment required to meet this standard will be severe (19:22).

The reason that a "divestment of surplus" must be considered normative stewardship for all followers of Jesus becomes clear when we consider the rationale that Jesus offers for not storing up treasures on earth. The problem is not just that such treasures are subject to the vagaries of moths, rust, and thieves but, more important, that "where your treasure is, there your heart will be also" (6:21). In articulating this principle, Jesus offers insight into a spiritual truth that will affect all who wish to serve God as their one master. Jesus discerns an inevitable link between accumulation of material possessions and devotion to them. Hence those who accumulate possessions are unable to love or serve God (6:24).

This rationale encourages readers to take the call to divestment in Matthew literally. Readers should realize that Jesus' demand cannot be met simply by renouncing their possessions in a spiritual sense, such as by setting priorities in life that limit devotion to material things. According to Jesus, this is not possible for mortals (19:26). Unless people actually get rid of their material possessions, the latter will determine their spiritual priorities. The tendency for one to become devoted to one's possessions, furthermore, increases proportionately with the number of possessions one has. When Matthew says the rich young man turns down Jesus' invitation to discipleship because he has "many possessions" (19:22), the implication is that he might have been able to respond favorably if only he had fewer possessions. This, of course, is why rich people are almost categorically excluded from the kingdom of heaven (19:23-24).

We must conclude, then, that, for Matthew, good stewardship with regard to material possessions normally requires divestment of all but the basic necessities of life and sometimes requires a divestment of virtually everything, such that even these necessities must be provided through the charity of others. When we consider Matthew's second principle of stewardship, however, we see that the issues can become more complicated than this initial conclusion would suggest. Acknowledging God as lord affects the attitude that people have toward material possessions in at least three ways.

First, since material blessings can be gifts of God, stewards must be careful not to despise them. True, life is "more than food, and the body more than clothing" (6:25), but both food and clothing are good things (7:11) given by God (6:25-30). Paradoxically intertwined with the endorsement of an austere lifestyle in Matthew's Gospel is a robust appreciation for what might be considered worldly by the ascetic. Called "a glutton and a drunkard" by his detractors (11:19), Jesus likens the reign of God to a marvelous feast (22:1-14; 25:10) and unabashedly speaks of monetary gifts (20:1-15; 25:14-30) and material rewards (24:47) as symbols of God's grace and bounty. The faithful steward, caught up in this paradox, must appreciate material blessings as God's gifts, while also taking care not to accumulate possessions or become devoted to them.

Second, acknowledgment of God as lord implies trust that God will provide what is needed. In Matthew's Gospel, serving mammon is parallel to being anxious about food, drink, and clothing (6:24-25). Giving up possessions, then, may not be enough to guarantee that one is a good steward with regard to material things. If people voluntarily adopt an austere lifestyle and then worry about what they will eat, drink, and wear instead of seeking God's reign and righteousness (6:33), they will fail to serve their one master as expected. Acknowledgment of God as lord of one's material possessions means that divestment is accompanied by faith in God's providence.

Finally, Matthew's second principle of stewardship also implies acceptance that God can do as God wishes with what truly belongs to God. This is the fundamental point made by the parable of the Laborers in the Vineyard (20:1-16). When some of the workers are frustrated that they are not treated as generously as others, the householder replies, "Am I not allowed to do what I choose with what belongs to me?" Thus, recognition that all things belong to God rules out envy on the part of good stewards, for God can give what is God's to any and all as God wishes.

Consideration of this last point prevents us from defining Matthew's concept of stewardship in an absolute sense. God can and sometimes does break God's own rules for what is normally expected. For example, we have seen that according to Matthew's

Gospel a rich person can no more enter the kingdom of heaven than a camel can pass through the eye of a needle (19:23). But then in Matthew 27:57 we suddenly encounter "a rich man from Arimathea, named Joseph, who was also a disciple of Jesus." How can such a thing be? Matthew's Gospel has prepared us for such an eventuality through its insistence that "for God all things are possible" (19:26). We may object that, according to this book's own concept of stewardship, Joseph's heart will be with his riches (6:21) and his discipleship will be in vain. But such objections are overruled by the acknowledgment that God can do as God wishes with what belongs to God. If God decides that *this* disciple shall remain rich in defiance of the normative call to divestment and austerity, then no faithful steward ought to challenge God's generosity (20:15).

According to Matthew's third stewardship principle, God's people ought to regard material possessions as resources that God trusts them to use as God wishes. Joseph of Arimathea does this by donating a tomb for Jesus' burial (27:58-60). In contrast, the religious leaders of Israel use their financial resources to secure Jesus' betrayal (26:14) and to bribe soldiers to lie about his resurrection (28:12-15).

Matthew's Gospel does not offer very much teaching on the responsible use of material possessions because the operating assumption is that the financial resources of people who are not concerned with storing up treasures on earth will be slight. The two uses that receive the most attention, charitable giving to the poor and the offering of gifts in worship, both represent instances in which material resources are simply given away with no thought of receiving anything tangible in return. Thus the theme of responsible use of possessions is closely tied to the theme of divestment discussed earlier.

Matthew's readers are expected to give to anyone who begs (5:42) and to give alms in ways that do not win glory for themselves (6:2-4). Charitable giving to the poor is also emphasized in Jesus' words to the rich young man (19:21). If this man would simply abandon his possessions in a manner comparable to that evidenced by Jesus' disciples (4:20, 22; 19:27), that would be sufficient to satisfy Matthew's first principle and assure that this potential disciple's heart would be devoted solely to God (6:19-21). But the specificity of Jesus' instructions indicate, once again, that this is not enough. What is called for is not just divestment but *redistribution*. To be perfect and have treasure in heaven good stewards must not only get rid of their possessions; they must give their money to the poor. As we observed in our discussion of human relationships, Matthew's stewardship principles are held together by the same logic that presents the commandments concerning love for God and neighbor as synonymous (22:34-40). The devotion for God that is effected through divestment of one's material possessions is one with the devotion to neighbor effected through charitable giving to the poor. Accordingly, Matthew explicitly presents one example of giving to the poor—providing support for ministers who work without pay (10:8)—as a means of displaying devotion to Jesus and to God (10:40-42; see also 25:31-46).

The story of the Magi illustrates another commendable use of material possessions, namely, the offering of gifts as a form of worship (2:11).[16] By giving their treasures to Jesus, the Magi commit their hearts to him as well (6:21). The story of the woman who anoints Jesus with expensive ointment is a parallel to this, for by emphasizing the great value of the ointment "wasted" on Jesus (26:8-9), Matthew indicates that her devotion is to him, not to money. Indeed, according to Matthew 6:21, dedication of financial resources always determines the commitment of one's heart, which is why responsible use of material possessions is so important. Matthew's Gospel does not teach that people will invest their treasure in things that matter to them ("Where your heart is, there your treasure will be") but vice versa ("Where your treasure is, there your heart will be"). Accordingly, faithful stewards do not just "give from the heart," that is, give according to where their hearts are now; rather, they strive to put their treasures where they hope their hearts will be in the future. The offering of gifts in worship would seem to be a prime example of such commitment.

In the story of the Magi and of the woman at Bethany, the gifts are presented directly to Jesus himself (2:11). Since such presentations are no longer possible for Matthew's readers, we may ask

16. On gift giving as a form of worship in Matthew, see the discussion in chap. 2 above, pp. 46–47.

how they are expected to offer gifts to Jesus in worship. As we have already noted, Matthew's Gospel affirms that what is done for others often counts as action performed for Jesus (10:40; 18:5; 25:35-40, 42-45). But with regard to financial offerings, Matthew also inherits a notion that was already commonplace within the Jewish milieu, namely, that gifts are offered to God when they are presented to a religious institution and used for the support of that institution. Matthew, however, consistently treats such offerings as a relatively low priority. Tithing is commendable, but it is less important than observance of the weightier matters of the law—justice and mercy and faith (23:23). Similarly, reconciliation between estranged members of the community must be regarded as a higher priority than presentation of gifts at the altar (5:23-24). Again, providing for one's parents is a financial responsibility that ought to take precedence over contributions to religious institutions (15:3-6).[17]

We may ask whether Matthew presents the financial support of religious institutions as a low stewardship priority because the institutions that figure in his story are corrupt ones. According to Matthew's Gospel, the religious leaders of Israel have come to view the gold of the temple as more sacred than the temple itself and to prize gifts presented there as greater than the altar on which they are placed (23:16-19). Commercialization of the temple is transforming it from a house of prayer into a den of thieves (21:12-13). But if such practices were completely devastating, Matthew would not present Jesus as commending support of the temple through tithes (23:23) and offerings (5:23-24) at all. As it is, Jesus claims that God dwells in the temple (23:21) and his attacks on abuses in the temple only confirm his support for the institution as a whole. Jesus himself contributes financially to the temple cult, even though he does not feel obligated to do so (17:24-27).

The point, rather, may be that giving gifts to religious institutions *as an expression of worship* has value beyond that associated with the support of these institutions per se. On the one hand, Matthew seems to regard the financial support of one's religious

---

17. The story of the widow who gives all that she has to the temple is not found in Matthew (see Mark 12:41-44; Luke 21:1-4).

institution as a social duty analogous to payment of taxes to the
government. The political and religious institutions in Matthew's story are both described as corrupted by ideas foreign to
the thinking of God, but Jesus endorses a basic financial support
of both nevertheless (17:24-27; 22:17-21). The offering of gifts
in worship, on the other hand, may secure the heart of the donor
in a way that the mere performance of a social duty would not
(6:21). Thus, even though support for religious institutions may
be regarded as a relatively low priority in and of itself, such support may take on an entirely new meaning and become much
more important when it is given as an expression of worship.
Even though their gifts are presented directly to Jesus rather
than to an institution, the Magi (2:11) and the woman with the
ointment (26:8-9) provide Matthew's readers with better models
for such giving than do the Pharisees, who do as they ought but
still miss the point (23:23).

With regard to financial giving, Matthew's Gospel always emphasizes the benefits to the givers rather than to the recipients.
Jesus does not direct the rich man to give to the poor because the
poor need his money but because the rich man himself needs to
become perfect and gain treasure in heaven (19:21). Likewise,
worshipers may be encouraged to give of their earthly treasures
not primarily because the religious institutions need their money
but because such giving frees the worshipers from servitude to
mammon and secures the devotion of their hearts to God as their
one master (6:21, 24).

CHAPTER FIVE

SOCIAL JUSTICE

ACCORDING TO THE GOSPEL OF MATTHEW, justice (*krisis*) is one of "the weightier matters of the law" (23:23). People are told to seek God's justice or righteousness (*dikaiosynē*) above all else (6:33), and those who do so are promised satisfaction (5:6). Still, Matthew's concept of *social* justice is often thought to be limited by a dualism that views the church rather than the world as the arena in which God's will is done. Such an understanding seems to be expressed in Matthew 20:25-26, where Jesus tells his disciples, "You know that the rulers of the Gentiles lord it over them. . . . It will not be so among you." Matthew's Gospel appears to grant that the justice it encourages will not be a reality in society as a whole but is to be practiced in the new communities of Jesus' followers.

The most popular text in Matthew for discussions of social justice is probably the "sheep and goats" account in 25:31-46.[1] But this text's popularity may derive from interpretations not supported by modern scholarship.[2] Popular references to Matthew 25:31-46 usually describe church members as being held accountable for how they respond to needy persons of the world, with whom Jesus identifies.[3] A careful reading of the text, however, reveals the expressed concern to be for those needy persons

1. For a survey of its interpretation and influence throughout history, see Sherman W. Gray, *The Least of My Brothers: Matthew 25:31-46: A History of Interpretation* (SBLDS 114; Atlanta: Scholars Press, 1989).

2. Cope, "Matthew xxv:31-46"; and Stanton, *Gospel for a New People*, 207–31.

3. Such interpretations are not without support from noted exegetes. See Meier, *Vision*, 77–78; Pheme Perkins, *Hearing the Parables of Jesus* (New York: Paulist Press, 1981), 158–65; and Schweizer, *Good News*, 480–84. They also tend

who may be described specifically as siblings (*adelphoi*) of Jesus. Elsewhere in Matthew, Jesus' siblings are identified with his disciples, with members of the community of faith (12:50; 18:15, 21). The scene depicted in 25:31-46 is most likely a judgment of non-Christians ("the nations") based on how they have responded to the Christian missionaries whom Jesus sends to them (28:19; compare 10:9-15, 40-43).[4] Even in this passage, then, the focus of Matthew's Gospel appears to be on justice for people within the community rather than on justice for people in the world at large.

Critics of Matthew's Gospel have sometimes objected to this concept of justice on grounds that it encourages detachment rather than involvement.[5] Others regard the focus on establishing justice within foundational, alternative communities to be a wise strategy, especially for Christians living in a society that does not recognize or respect the contributions of their religion.[6]

The goal of this chapter is neither to condemn nor to defend Matthew's concept of social justice but to describe it as accurately as possible. We will examine Matthew's key terms for justice and will discuss two passages that I have come to regard as foundational for understanding Matthew's social ethic. While such an investigation is far from exhaustive, it will be sufficient to demonstrate that Matthew's vision of social justice is more complex than traditional notions have allowed.

---

to be favored by liberation theologians, such as Gustavo Gutiérrez, *The Theology of Liberation* (Maryknoll, N.Y.: Orbis Books, 1973), 198.

4. Against this, two points are raised: (*a*) those who are judged call Jesus "Lord" (*kyrios*, 25:37, 44), a term that elsewhere in Matthew is used only by those who are at least ostensibly people of faith (7:21-22; 8:2, 6, 8, 21, 25; 9:28; 14:28, 30; 15:22, 25, 27; 16:22; 17:4, 15; 18:21; 20:30-31, 33). But for Matthew the final judgment is a time when those who have not previously recognized or acknowledged Jesus will see him for who he is (24:30; 27:64); (*b*) the account comes at the end of a section in Matthew that describes a coming judgment of the church. But the passage can easily be understood as an expansion on this theme, indicating that the final judgment will not be limited to the church.

5. Jack T. Sanders, *Ethics in the New Testament* (Philadelphia: Fortress Press, 1975), 40–46.

6. Crosby, *House of Disciples*.

KEY WORDS

The concept of justice is a broad one,[7] and Matthew's Gospel does not appear to subscribe to any single theory or school of thought on the subject.[8] The Gospel uses terms for justice without defining them, but some preliminary observations on the most important of these terms will provide orientation for understanding what is meant by justice in this book.

1. *Dikaiosynē* occurs seven times in Matthew's Gospel (3:15; 5:6, 10, 20; 6:1; 6:33; 21:32) and may be translated as "righteousness" (KJV, NASB, NIV, NRSV, RSV), "uprightness" (NJB), or "what God requires" (TEV).[9] Many English versions vary their usual translation at 6:1, such that Jesus warns against the public practice of "good deeds" (JB), "alms" (KJV), "religion" (NEB, REB), "piety" (NRSV, RSV), or "religious duties" (TEV). In addition, some versions render *dikaiosynē* in 6:33 as "justice" (NEB, REB) or "saving justice" (NJB). The adjective *dikaios* is used eighteen times[10] (often substantivally) and is typically translated "righteous" or "just."

Two observations are pertinent concerning the generic meaning of *dikaiosynē* and *dikaios*.[11] First, the terms express a basic concept of appropriateness. In one Matthean parable, an owner of a vineyard offers to pay the workers "whatever is *dikaios,*" that is, whatever is appropriate (20:4). So the very use of these terms assumes the conviction that there is a way that things ought to be, and that things may be described as either being or not being the way they ought to be. Second, the concept of *dikaiosynē* is inherently relational. Nothing is *dikaios* in and of

---

7. Karen Lebacqz, *Six Theories of Justice: Perspectives from Philosophical and Theological Ethics* (Minneapolis: Augsburg Publishing House, 1986).

8. Cain Felder defines four types of early Christian justice articulated in the New Testament and illustrates three of these with material from Matthew. See Cain H. Felder, "Toward a New Testament Hermeneutic for Justice," *JRT* 45 (1988): 10–27.

9. NEB and REB are idiosyncratic, translating *dikaiosynē* differently every single time it occurs and omitting it altogether in 5:20.

10. 1:19; 5:45; 9:13; 10:41 (twice); 13:17, 43, 49; 20:4; 23:28, 29, 35 (twice); 25:37, 46; 27:4, 19, 24.

11. *EDNT*, 1:324–30; and *TDNT*, 2:182–210.

itself, but things are *dikaios* when they are rightly related to each other. Matthew's Gospel instills *dikaiosynē* with specific religious content. In Matthew, things are the way they ought to be when they are the way God wants them to be, and people[12] are "righteous" or "just" when they are rightly related to God. With regard to the latter point, though, we must recall what was said in the previous chapter (pp. 102–03), namely, that being rightly related to God implies right relations with everything else, including one's possessions (6:24), one's neighbors (22:38-40), and even one's enemies (5:44).

Matthew's Gospel speaks sometimes of the *dikaiosynē* of God and at other times of the *dikaiosynē* of people.[13] A clear example of the former is 6:33, where God's *dikaiosynē* is presented as a correlate to God's *basileia* (kingdom). Here, the righteousness or justice of God may be defined as the state of affairs that transpires when God rules. Matthew 5:20, however, speaks not of the *dikaiosynē* of God but of the *dikaiosynē* of Jesus' disciples. From the context, this *dikaiosynē* may be defined as faithfulness in teaching and doing the commandments of God's law (5:19). Whereas in 6:33 *dikaiosynē* refers to conditions established by God, in 5:20 it refers to conduct expected by God.

In some cases, Matthew's Gospel does not specify whether the *dikaiosynē* referred to in the text is that of God or of people. What does Jesus mean, for instance, when he says that John the Baptist came "in the way of *dikaiosynē*" (21:32)? Does he mean that John came as God's agent, helping to usher in the rule of God so that things will be as they ought? Or does he mean that John came as one who was himself righteous or just, a per-

12. Aside from 20:4, human beings are always the expressed or implied referent for *dikaios* in Matthew's Gospel. "Righteous blood" (23:35; 27:4) means "the blood of a righteous person."

13. Scholars have debated as to whether *dikaiosynē* in Matthew might always refer either to God's gift or to human obedience. For bibliography of these extreme views and convincing arguments as to why the term must encompass both senses, see John P. Meier, *Law and History in Matthew* (AnBib 71; Rome: Biblical Institute, 1976), 76–79; and John Reumann, *Righteousness in the New Testament* (Philadelphia: Fortress Press, 1982), 125–35.

son who faithfully observed the law and demanded that others do so? Either interpretation may be consistent with the portrayal of John in Matthew's narrative (3:1-17; 11:7-15), so we must allow for ambiguity. The two senses of this term are not contradictory but expressive of the inherently relational concept that *dikaiosynē* describes. References to the *dikaiosynē* of God emphasize the divine contribution to the relationship, while references to the *dikaiosynē* of people emphasize the human component. Sometimes, furthermore, Matthew's Gospel employs the term in contexts that emphasize the activity either of God or of humans while assuming (but not emphasizing) the activity of the other. In 6:33 the conditions that will be established by God are something that people ought to seek, and in 5:20 the conduct expected by God is predicated on the coming of Jesus to fulfill the law and the prophets (5:17). Far from being mutually exclusive, the two senses of *dikaiosynē* appear in Matthew to be inherently complementary.

In any case, *dikaiosynē* in Matthew is an essentially eschatological phenomenon.[14] Both components of what Matthew calls *dikaiosynē* are contained in Jesus' central pronouncement, "Repent, for the kingdom of heaven has come near" (3:2; 4:17). The *dikaiosynē* of God is evidenced by the imminence of the kingdom, and the *dikaiosynē* of God's people is demonstrated when they respond to that imminence with repentance.

2. *Krisis* occurs twelve times in Matthew (5:21, 22; 10:15; 11:22, 24; 12:18, 20, 36, 41, 42; 23:23, 33). Of these instances, nine refer clearly to a time of judgment when the wicked will be punished for their sins. In three cases, however, the word is used with a different sense. Jesus is identified as the one whom the prophet Isaiah said would proclaim *krisis* to the Gentiles and who would bring *krisis* to victory (12:18, 20; compare Isa 42:1-4). Also, in 23:23, Jesus tells the scribes and the Pharisees that they have neglected the weightier matters of the law, *krisis* and mercy (*eleos*) and faith (*pistis*). Although most English Bibles translate *krisis* as "judgment" in the nine instances that refer to a time of

14. Nlenanya Onwu, "Righteousness and Eschatology in Matthew's Gospel: A Critical Reflection," *ITS* 25 (1988): 213–35.

recompense, many prefer to use "justice" in the other three instances.[15]

The distinctive uses of *krisis* in Matthew 12:18-20 and 23:23 derive from the LXX, where the word is regularly used to translate *mishpat*. The references in 12:18-20 are drawn explicitly from the Old Testament (Isa 42:1-4), and the pairing of *krisis* with *eleos* in 23:23 recalls LXX Ps 101:1 (English, 100:1). Throughout the LXX, *krisis* is used to refer to "what is right," with special emphasis on vindication of the oppressed.[16] The connection between "justice" and "judgment" (*mishpat* is used for both concepts in the Old Testament) lies in the conviction that the former is established through the latter. Ideally, the decision of a judge brings about what is right, including vindication of the oppressed. Judgment is the means and justice is the end.

In Matthew's narrative, the judgment that brings justice is clearly that of God. As the other uses of *krisis* indicate, this judgment is essentially eschatological. On the "day of judgment" God's decision will take effect and put all things right. Still, the references to *krisis* in 12:18-20 and 23:23 indicate that this judgment is already becoming a present reality. The presentation of Jesus as one who proclaims (God's) judgment (12:18) is congruent with the portrayal of him as one who announces, "The kingdom of heaven has come near" (4:17). In both cases, Jesus is declaring that God rules already, here and now. Just as Jesus' exorcisms demonstrate that "the kingdom of God has come to you" (12:28), so his healings are evidence that he is bringing God's judgment (*krisis*) to victory (12:20; see also 12:15). God's rule decisively eliminates such things as sickness and demonic possession.

Matthew 12:18-20 represents *krisis*, the judgment that brings justice, as something that God establishes. Yet in Matthew 23:23 Jesus upbraids the scribes and the Pharisees because they have neglected *krisis*. God's people, then, are not just expected to wait passively for God to put things right. Rather, like Jesus, they ought to be proclaiming God's decisions right now and putting

---

15. KJV uses "judgment" in 12:18, 20; 23:23; NJB uses "judgment" in 12:18, 20; NEB and TEV use "judgment" in 12:18 alone. JB favors the idiosyncratic readings of "true faith" in 12:18 and "the truth" in 12:20.

16. *TDNT*, 3:941–42.

them into effect. The scribes and the Pharisees have failed to do this because they "make void the word of God," teaching instead what are merely human precepts (15:6, 9).

Conclusion. From what has been said, we may gather that *dikaiosynē* and *krisis* (as it is used in 12:18-20 and 23:23) are synonyms in Matthew's Gospel. At root, *dikaiosynē* carries a stronger nuance of "right relationships" and *krisis* more of an emphasis on "the decision that vindicates," but even these distinctions become blurred in application. In Matthew, both terms carry a primary sense of "what is right." Both terms are also given content that is entirely religious and specifically eschatological. According to Matthew's Gospel, justice (the way things ought to be) is something that must be established by God, but it is also something that *is being* established by God to an extent that now demands human recognition and participation.

THE BEATITUDES

Matthew 5:3-12 is widely recognized as a passage of exceptional significance for Matthean theology.[17] As the opening words of the Sermon on the Mount, these verses provide a foundation for understanding the core of Jesus' ethical instruction. We should not be surprised, then, to find that the passage is also foundational for defining Matthew's views on social justice.

Contemporary scholars debate whether Matthew's beatitudes intend to promise eschatological rewards for the virtuous or eschatological reversals for the unfortunate.[18] Two distinct ap-

17. Warren Kissinger lists over three hundred studies on the beatitudes, all of which were published prior to 1975. See Warren S. Kissinger, *The Sermon on the Mount: A History of Interpretation and Bibliography* (Metuchen, N.J.: Scarecrow Press, 1975), 242–75. On the exegetical basis for this section, see my forthcoming article in the *Catholic Biblical Quarterly*, "Matthew's Beatitudes: Reversals and Rewards of the Kingdom."

18. For bibliography and summary of the debate, see W. D. Davies and Dale C. Allison, *A Critical and Exegetical Commentary on the Gospel according to Saint Matthew*, 3 vols. (ICC; Edinburgh: T. & T. Clark, 1988, 1991, forthcoming), 1:439–40; Robert A. Guelich, *The Sermon on the Mount: A Foundation for Understanding* (Waco, Tex.: Word Books, 1982), 109–11; and Ulrich Luz, *Matthew 1–7: A Continental Commentary*, trans. Wilhelm C. Linss (CC; 1989; reprint, Minneapolis: Fortress Press, 1992), 229–30.

proaches have been taken: (1) Some determined interpreters try
to fit all the beatitudes into one scheme or the other,[19] although
notorious problem passages arise either way. Mourning (5:4), for
instance, does not sound like a virtue to which we should all
aspire, nor do peacemakers (5:9) sound like an unfortunate class
of people who need to have their situation reversed. This approach, although popular, has been unsuccessful at producing an
interpretation of the beatitudes that does justice to the individual
verses. The interpretive grid imposed on the unit as a whole inevitably demands that some verses be read in a way that seems
forced or strained. (2) Some scholars are willing to sacrifice con-
sistency for the unit as a whole in order to interpret each beatitude on its own terms.[20] Beatitudes that promise rewards for the
virtuous and ones that promise reversals for the unfortunate have
been gathered together in a collection that appears more coher-
ent than it really is. This approach has succeeded where the first
has failed but has, in turn, been unsuccessful at producing a
meaningful interpretation for the beatitudes as a unit. The poetic
structure of the beatitudes predisposes Matthew's readers to
expect a pattern reminiscent of Hebrew parallelism. In many
ways, the beatitudes are the most beautifully crafted passage in
Matthew's Gospel. Thus, unless no other option exists, Matthew's readers should not be forced to decide between finding
meaning for the individual verses and finding meaning for the
collection as a whole.

A third option may be suggested by studies on the structure of
the Matthean beatitudes. Almost all interpreters recognize that
Matthew 5:3-10 is a structural unit that must be considered apart
from Matthew 5:11-12.[21] The eight beatitudes in verses 3-10 are

---

19. Those who read them as promising rewards include Jacques Dupont,
Les béatitudes, 3 vols. (Paris: J. Gabalda, 1969, 1969, 1973); Georg Strecker,
"Die Makarismen der Bergpredigt," *NTS* 17 (1970/71): 255–75; and Hans
Windisch, *The Meaning of the Sermon on the Mount*, trans. S. MacLean Gilmour
(Philadelphia: Westminster Press, 1951). Those who read them as promising
reversals include Davies and Allison; Guelich.

20. For an example of such an approach, see Luz, who thinks "it is unlikely
that there is for Matthew a unified religious or ethical meaning" even in the
first four beatitudes (p. 235).

21. The one notable exception is Davies and Allison (pp. 429–31), whose
arguments for a tripartite outline (5:3-5, 6-8, 9-12) have convinced few. Other

all addressed in the third person and are held together by the redundant apodoses of the first and last in the series. Verses 11-12, on the other hand, are addressed in the second person and are distinguished from the preceding verses by length, meter, and use of the imperative mood. Beyond this obvious division, many scholars also contend that Matthew 5:3-10 should be subdivided into two stanzas with four lines apiece.[22] Both Matthew 5:3-6 and 5:7-10 contain exactly thirty-six words (5:11-12 contains thirty-five), the protoses of 5:6 and 5:10 both conclude with the word *dikaiosynē*, and 5:3-6 exhibits internal alliteration through the naming of groups that begin with the letter *p*: the poor (*ptōchoi*) in spirit, those who mourn (*penthountes*), the meek (*praeis*), and those who hunger (*peinontes*) and thirst for righteousness.[23] If these arguments are not completely convincing on their own, they at least raise the possibility of a subdivision.

With regard to parallelism, the greatest argument for subdividing Matthew 5:3-10 into two stanzas is length. I know of no example of eight-line synonymous parallelism in Hebrew poetry, but four-line parallels are possible. Furthermore, although attempts at reading all eight (or nine) beatitudes according to one consistent scheme have proved unsuccessful, the verses that are the most irreconcilable according to such a scheme do not occur within the same set of four when Matthew 5:3-10 is subdivided. Thus, reasonable parallels can be maintained for the four beatitudes in the first set and for the four in the second set if each of

---

non-traditional outlines for the beatitudes include a chiastic structure suggested by Neil J. McEleney, "The Beatitudes of the Sermon on the Mount/Plain," *CBQ* 43 (1981): 1–13, and an aural structure presented in Bernard Brandon Scott and Margaret E. Dean, "A Sound Map of the Sermon on the Mount," in *SBL 1993 Seminar Papers*, ed. Eugene H. Lovering, Jr. (Atlanta: Scholars Press, 1993), 672–725, esp. 680–82. But even the latter two proposals recognize the distinction between 5:3-10 and 5:11-12.

22. Gundry, 73; Jan Lambrecht, *The Sermon on the Mount: Proclamation and Exhortation* (GNS 14; Wilmington, Del.: Michael Glazier, 1989), 61; Luz, 226; John P. Meier, *Matthew* (NTM 3; Collegeville, Minn.: Liturgical Press, 1980), 39; Christine Michaelis, "Die *p*-Alliteration der Subjektworte der ersten 4 Seligpreisungen in Mt v 3-6 und ihre Bedeutung für den Aufbau der Seligpreisungen bei Mt, Lk, und in Q," *NovT* 10 (1968): 148–61; and Schweizer, *Good News*, 82.

23. On the latter point, see Michaelis.

these two sets is treated as a separate stanza.[24] Our analysis, then, shall assume the following outline: First Stanza (5:3-6); Second Stanza (5:7-10); Concluding Comment (5:11-12).

First Stanza. All four of the beatitudes in the first stanza may reasonably be interpreted as promising eschatological reversals to those who are unfortunate, and some of the beatitudes in this stanza can be reasonably interpreted only in this way. Some commentators have identified the *poor in spirit* in 5:3 as referring to people who are "humble,"[25] and a few have even taken it as a reference to those who renounce their possessions in order to be "voluntarily poor."[26] In either case, the poor in spirit are regarded as virtuous persons who are given the kingdom of heaven as a reward for their humility or voluntary poverty. A majority of modern scholars, however, identify Matthew's poor in spirit with the *anawim*, that is, with the dispossessed and abandoned ones in Israel, on whose behalf the prophets speak (Isa 11:4; 29:19; 32:7; 61:1; Amos 2:7; 8:4; Zeph 2:3).[27] A few scholars

24. Uniformity in content for 5:3-6 and 5:7-10 is noted by Gundry; Lambrecht, *Sermon*; Luz; Meier, *Matthew*; Michaelis; and Schweizer, *Good News*. The first set refers to (passive) conditions and the second to (active) behavior or attitudes. Guelich (p. 115) thinks the first four beatitudes are aligned with Isaiah 61. Even Windisch (*Meaning*, 175–77), who takes all eight as promising rewards, speaks of two series, one offering consolation and the other clarifying expectations. A nontechnical work by Gene Davenport discusses 5:1-6 under the rubric "Blessings on the Victimized" and 5:7-12 under "Blessings on the Faithful." See Gene L. Davenport, *Into the Darkness: Discipleship in the Sermon on the Mount* (Nashville: Abingdon Press, 1988). Hagner thinks that attitude is primary for the first four and conduct for the second four. See Donald Hagner, *Matthew 1–13* (WBC; Dallas: Word Books, 1993), 93.

25. Dupont, 3:462–65, 470–71; S. Légasse, "Les pauvres en esprit et les 'volontaires' de Qumran," *NTS* 8 (1962): 336–45; Thaddäus Soiron, *Die Bergpredigt Jesu* (Freiburg: Herder, 1941), 146–47; and Georg Strecker, *The Sermon on the Mount: An Exegetical Commentary*, trans. O. C. Dean (Nashville: Abingdon Press, 1988), 31–32. Most of the early "church fathers" understood the term this way—see Dupont, 3:399–411; and Luz, 234–35.

26. Ernst Lohmeyer, *Das Evangelium des Matthäus*, 2d ed. (Göttingen: Vandenhoeck & Ruprecht, 1958), 82–83; K. Schubert, "The Sermon on the Mount and the Qumran Texts," in *The Scrolls and the New Testament*, ed. Krister Stendahl (London: SCM Press, 1957).

27. For a sampling, see Guelich, 66–75; Hagner, *Matthew 1–13*, 91–92; Dennis Hamm, *The Beatitudes in Context: What Luke and Matthew Meant*

think that to be poor in spirit means to be "fainthearted" or "despondent."[28] In either of the latter cases, the beatitude promises a reversal of unfortunate conditions rather than a reward.

Association of the poor in spirit with the *anawim* is surely correct, but the Old Testament concept provides only a background against which Matthew's particular interests must also be considered. In the Old Testament, the *anawim* appear to be a socioeconomic class within Israel who are noted as much for their piety as for their poverty. The general thought seems to be that they trust in God more profoundly than most because they have no hope in this world.[29] The poor in spirit referred to in Matthew 5:3 are like the *anawim* in that they too have no hope in this world, but Matthew's concept of the poor in spirit may differ from the Old Testament concept of the *anawim* in two ways.

First, Matthean universalism makes identification of the poor in spirit with a group internal to Israel unlikely. Matthew's readers are expected to note that those who hear these beatitudes are called "the salt of the *earth*" (5:13) and "the light of the *world*" (5:14). Likewise, Jesus is identified as one who proclaims justice to the *Gentiles* (12:18) and as one in whose name these Gentiles will hope (12:21). In the context of Matthew's Gospel, then, "poor in spirit" ought to be taken as a reference that expands on the *anawim* of the Old Testament to include the dispossessed and abandoned people of the world in general.

Second, Matthew's use of the phrase "in spirit" qualifies the notion of the *anawim* in a way that emphasizes the negative spiritual consequences of poverty. Notably, the term *ptōchoi* ("poor") alone is used to translate *anawim* in the LXX (Isa 29:19; 61:1). The additional words "in spirit," then, bring out the notion of despondency[30] or loss of hope. Whereas in the Old Testament

(Wilmington, Del.: Michael Glazier, 1990), 80–81; Hill, 110–11; Meier, *Matthew*, 39–40; Schweizer, *Good News*, 86–87.

28. Ernest Best, "Matthew V-3," *NTS* 7 (1960/61): 255–58.

29. *ABD*, 5:411–13. See also Hans-Joachim Kraus, *Theology of the Psalms: A Continental Commentary*, trans. K. Crim (CC; 1986; reprint, Minneapolis: Fortress Press, 1992), 150–54.

30. Best interprets this despondency as an understandable reaction to the harsh demands of Jesus' sermon, an interpretation that fails to note any connection to the *anawim* and that ignores the use of the third person by assuming that the beatitude refers to those to whom Jesus is speaking.

the *anawim* are represented as people who have an unusually strong hope (in God), the accent on spiritual poverty here redefines them as people who may be on the verge of giving up. Thus, in Matthew's Gospel the poor in spirit are not people who trust in God because they have no reason for hope in this world. They are people who have no reason for hope in this world, period. The presence or strength of their trust in God remains unaddressed in this beatitude, although, if anything, the implication of the Matthean phrase would be that it is slight.[31]

The poor in spirit are declared blessed because "of them is the kingdom of heaven" (*autōn estin hē basileia tōn houranōn*). English translations often render this as a possessive: "theirs is the kingdom of heaven." Matthew's Gospel does contain parables that liken the kingdom to an object (a treasure or a pearl) that one might obtain (13:44-46), but such imagery may ultimately fail to do justice to the sovereignty of God's rule central to this Gospel's theology. The real sense of the apodosis of this beatitude (see also 5:10; 19:14) may be brought out by taking the two genitive constructions as objective and subjective complements of a verbal noun. The phrase then reads simply, "heaven rules them."

As indicated above, *those who mourn* (5:4) must be taken as a reference to unfortunate persons in need of reversal rather than to virtuous ones deserving a reward. Commentators who think Matthew refers to people who are "sorry for their sins"[32] or who "protest evil and injustice"[33] or who "renounce earthly goods"[34] are straining for applications that Matthew's readers would not be expected to deduce from the text. Such desperation is unnecessary apart from a predisposition toward finding promises of

31. Most interpreters who identify 5:3 as a reference to the *anawim* think the addition of the words "in spirit" intensifies the already implicit characterization of these persons as religious or pious. Such interpretations are curious, for they appear to assume that Matthew is referring to those who are spiritually *rich* in spite of their socioeconomic poverty.

32. Hugo Huber, *Die Bergpredigt* (Göttingen: Vandenhoeck & Ruprecht, 1932), 29–31. According to Luz (p. 235 n. 64), this view has been prevalent since Origen.

33. Bruce J. Malina, *Christian Origins and Cultural Anthropology: Practical Models for Biblical Interpretation* (Atlanta: John Knox Press, 1986), 203.

34. Most notably, Augustine, *Commentary on the Lord's Sermon on the Mount*, 1.5.

reward in all the beatitudes. Most recent scholars recognize that "those who mourn" refers simply to people who are miserable or unhappy.[35] In its most specific sense, *pentheō* refers to grief related to death or loss, but the term may be used inclusively for sorrow in general. The mention of mourning (*pentheō*) and comfort (*parakaleō*) in this verse recalls Isa 61:1-3, which in the LXX also speaks of the poor (*ptōchoi*) and of those with a faint spirit (*pneumatos akēdias*). If the poor in spirit are those who find no reason for hope in this life, then the ones who mourn are those who find no cause for joy. They are blessed because "they will be comforted," a divine passive that implies God will act, so they need mourn no more.

Most interpreters regard *the meek* (*praüs*) in 5:5 as an approximate synonym for the "poor in spirit" of 5:3.[36] As such, the meek have been identified as people who are "humble,"[37] with perhaps a nuance of "nonviolent"[38] or "gentle."[39] Once again, however, many interpreters identify the meek here with the *anawim* of the Old Testament.[40] The case for doing so is at least as strong here as in 5:3 because the word *praüs* is the term most commonly used in the LXX to translate *anawim*. As Klaus Wengst has shown in a book-length word study of this term,[41] the connotation of *praüs* as "gentle" or "kind" derives from Greco-Roman literature and may be reflected in 1 Peter 3:4 (the only occurrence of the term in the New Testament outside of Matthew). In Matthew 5:5,

35. Davies and Allison, 448; Guelich, 79–81; Luz, 235. For Hagner (*Matthew 1–13*, 92), those who mourn are "those who suffer" and they do so "because of the seeming slowness of God's justice."

36. G. R. Beasley-Murray, *Jesus and the Kingdom of God* (Grand Rapids: Wm. B. Eerdmans, 1986), 158. Gundry (p. 69) traces the synonymity to an interplay between the Hebrew words for poor (*ani*) and meek (*anaw*).

37. Luz, 236.

38. Schalom Ben-Chorin, *Bruder Jesus*, 2d ed. (Munich: Paul List, 1969), 71.

39. Ambrose defined meekness as suppression of passion (*In Luc.* 5.54) and Gregory of Nyssa defined it as suppression of wrath (*De Beatitudinibus*, 2.3). So also Meier (*Matthew*, 40) thinks the meek are "the considerate, the unassuming, the peaceable toward God and man." Cf. Strecker, *Sermon*, 35–36.

40. Davies and Allison, 449; Guelich, 81–82; Hamm, 86–92; Hill, 11; Schweizer, *Good News*, 89–90.

41. Klaus Wengst, *Humility: Solidarity of the Humiliated*, trans. John Bowden (Philadelphia: Fortress Press, 1988).

however, the word ought to be interpreted in the Hebraic sense, for this verse is a near-quotation of LXX Psalm 36:11 (English, 37:11). Matthew's other two uses of the term also reflect Old Testament rootage. In 21:5 it is used in a citation from Zechariah, and in 11:29 it is combined with *tapeinos* ("lowly") in a pairing familiar to the LXX (for example, Zeph 3:12). As Wengst demonstrates, *praüs* does not refer to "the humble" in such instances but to "the humiliated."[42] Thus, the trend in recent scholarship has been toward identifying the *praüs* in Matthew 5:5 as "the oppressed" or "the powerless."[43]

Such an identification becomes even more likely when we consider the apodosis of this beatitude, the promise that the *praüs* will inherit the "earth" or "land" (*gēs*). In the Old Testament, both exodus and exile traditions speak of the disinherited (slaves, captives) receiving promised land (Hebrew, *eres*; LXX, *gēs*) in great reversals brought about by God. No biblical precedent indicates that the land is given as a reward to people who exhibit such virtues as kindness or gentleness. The very word "inherit" (*klēronomeō*) connotes not a reward that one must earn but a gift for which one must only wait. The sense of the third beatitude, then, is that dispossessed people are now regarded as blessed because they are going to receive what they have had coming to them all along. The reference to *gēs*, furthermore, helps to identify just what the *praüs* are envisioned as lacking. This time, it is something more worldly than hope or joy. The *praüs* are ones who have not been given their share of the earth. They have been denied access to the world's resources and have not had opportunity to enjoy the creation that God intended for all people.

The blessing pronounced on *those who hunger and thirst for righteousness/justice* in Matthew 5:6 may be interpreted as either a promise of reward for the virtuous or as a promise of reversal for the unfortunate. When the verse is taken in isolation, apart from any consideration of the beatitudes as a structural unit, the deciding factor for its interpretation will be the nuance attributed

---

42. Ibid. The emphasis in 11:29 and 21:5, then, is not on the pious personality of Jesus but on his voluntary identification with the lowly. See esp. pp. 36–41.

43. Davies and Allison, 449; Hagner, *Matthew 1–13*, 92–93; Schweizer, *Good News*, 89.

to *dikaiosynē* ("righteousness/justice"). As we have seen, this relational term is sometimes used in Matthew in a way that emphasizes the conduct of humans expected by God (5:20). Thus, a number of interpreters believe Matthew 5:6 refers to people who long to live according to God's will.[44] The term may also be used, however, with an emphasis on God's righteousness (6:33), that is, in reference to the activity of God that establishes justice. Many commentators think this is the sense implied by Matthew 5:6, such that the verse now refers to those who long for God to put things right,[45] indeed to those who long for vindication.[46]

Although this verse is ambiguous when not interpreted as part of a structural unit, a number of considerations favor placing the accent on people who desire conditions that will be established by God rather than on people who want their conduct to conform to what God expects. First, the closest parallel to the saying in Matthew's Gospel is 6:33, where the *dikaiosynē* to be sought by humans is identified as the state of affairs that transpires when God rules. Second, the concept of longing to do God's will is actually somewhat foreign to Matthew's Gospel, which values practice over intention (21:28-31; compare Rom 7:14-25). Third, the metaphors of hunger and thirst signify not only desire but also

44. Bornkamm, "End Expectation," 31; Davies and Allison, 451–53; Dupont, 3:361–64; Hill, 112; Luz, 237–38; Benno Przybylski, *Righteousness in Matthew and His World of Thought* (Cambridge: Cambridge University Press, 1980), 96–98; Alexander Sand, *Das Gesetz und die Propheten: Untersuchungen zur Theologie des Evangeliums nach Matthäus* (BU 11; Regensburg: Verlag Friedrich Pustet, 1974), 202; and Strecker, 37–38.

45. Jack Dean Kingsbury, *Matthew as Story*, 2d ed. (Philadelphia: Fortress Press, 1988), 132; Hagner, *Matthew 1–13*, 93; Lohmeyer, 87–88; Meier, *Matthew*, 40–41; Reumann, *Righteousness*, 127–28; Schweizer, *Good News*, 91–92; and Soiron, 171–72. Guelich (84–87) and others cited by him try to combine both elements by speaking of the desire for a fulfillment of God's will to be brought about by humans and by God.

46. Pierre Bonnard, *L'Évangile selon saint Matthieu*, 2d ed. (Neuchâtel: Delachaux & Niestlé, 1963), 57; Georg Eichholz, *Auslegung der Bergpredigt* (Neukirchen-Vluyn: Neukirchener Verlag, 1965), 43–44; Walter Grundmann, *Das Evangelium nach Matthäus* (THKNT 1; Berlin: Evangelische Verlagsanstalt, 1968), 126–27; Julius Schniewind, *Das Evangelium nach Matthäus*, 12th ed. (NTD 2; Göttingen: Vandenhoeck & Ruprecht, 1968), 44; Hans-Theo Wrege, *Die Überlieferungsgeschichte der Bergpredigt* (WUNT 9; Tübingen: J. C. B. Mohr, 1968), 19.

deprivation and the latter connotation makes more sense if we envision people who long for vindication rather than simply desiring to do what is right themselves. And, fourth, the expansion of this metaphor to include satisfaction of hunger and thirst connotes provision for basic needs rather than reward. Elsewhere in Matthew, satisfaction of hunger and thirst serves not as a symbol for eschatological reward but as an image of God's overall concern for creation (6:25-26). Indeed, Matthew's Gospel affirms that provision of life's basic necessities reflects the goodness of God in a way that is not contingent on the *dikaiosynē* of humans (5:45).

The best argument, however, for taking Matthew's fourth beatitude as a promise of reversal rather than reward is our recognition that it is parallel to the three beatitudes that precede it. As such, it functions as the concluding line of a stanza and sums up the thought of the entire unit thus far. Those who hunger and thirst for a justice that has been denied them include people who have no reason for hope, no cause for joy, and no access to the resources of this world. Such needs will be satisfied by the eschatological reversals that God's rule brings.

In short, the first four beatitudes speak of reversal of circumstances for those who are unfortunate. Contrary to popular homiletical treatments, being poor in spirit, mourning, being meek, and hungering and thirsting for righteousness/justice are not presented here as characteristics that people should exhibit if they want to earn God's favor.[47] Rather, these are undesirable conditions that characterize no one when God's will is done. The tendency to read Matthew's beatitudes as a catalog of virtues is so pervasive, however, that even commentators who agree that these beatitudes speak of reversals rather than rewards sometimes try to sneak a little virtue in through the back door. Thus, the poor in spirit may be regarded as the "religious poor," those who mourn may be identified as righteous people who suffer when the wicked prosper, the meek may become Christians who are powerless in an oppressive society, and so on. Nothing in the text

47. Nor are they presented as "character traits . . . which result from God's approval." David L. Turner, "Whom Does God Approve? The Context, Structure, Purpose, and Exegesis of Matthew's Beatitudes," *CTR* 6 (1992): 29–42, esp. 30.

of Matthew supports such specificity of identification. These beatitudes refer only to the circumstances of the unfortunate ones whom Jesus calls blessed. They do not describe the attitudes of those persons.

The desire of exegetes to identify the blessed in Matthew 5:3-6 with religious people or faithful Christians may be motivated by a common but erroneous assumption. Many interpreters assume that Jesus is referring here to his own disciples who in Matthew's Gospel serve as ciphers for "the church" (16:18; 18:17). Though Jesus addresses these words to the disciples (5:1-2), the use of the third person implies a distinction between those to whom Jesus is speaking and the people whom he describes as blessed. This distinction is emphasized when Jesus suddenly switches to the second person in his concluding comment in 5:11-12, the only one of the beatitudes that is conditional ("Blessed are you when . . .").

Some interpreters also think Matthew's Gospel would not be likely to include blessings for people of the world in general, since elsewhere it indicates that those who find the way of life are few (7:14). Indeed, God's ultimate gift of eschatological salvation may be reserved only for those who acknowledge God's Son (10:32-33) and do the will of the Father in heaven (7:21). But Matthew's Gospel also affirms that some of God's blessings are for all people, be they good or evil, righteous or unrighteous (5:45). The main point of the latter affirmation is to reveal the character of God and the nature of God's will.

Theologically, then, the point of these first four beatitudes is not to offer "entrance requirements for the kingdom of heaven"[48] but to describe the nature of God's rule, which characterizes the kingdom of heaven. Previously, John the Baptist and Jesus have declared that the kingdom of heaven has come near (3:2; 4:17), and Matthew has described this announcement as "good news" (*euaggelion*, 4:23). Now, in these beatitudes, Jesus' disciples learn for whom the announcement is good news. The people who benefit when God rules, Jesus declares, are those who otherwise have no reason for hope or cause for joy, who have

48. This persistent label was first applied to them by Hans Windisch in *Der Sinn der Bergpredigt*, although the exact phrase does not actually appear in the English translation of his work (*Meaning*, 88 n. 31).

been denied their share of God's blessings in this world and deprived of justice—in short, people for whom things have not
been the way they ought to be. For such people, the coming of
God's kingdom is a blessing, because when God rules, all this will
change and things will be set right.

Second Stanza. With the fifth beatitude of Matthew's Gospel
the pattern of parallelism is broken and a second set of parallels is
introduced. All of the beatitudes in Matthew 5:7-10 are best interpreted as promising eschatological rewards to people who exhibit virtuous behavior. The second stanza does not, however,
represent a logical departure from the thought that undergirds
the first, for the virtues that earn blessings are ones exercised on
behalf of the people mentioned in Stanza One. In other words,
the people whom Jesus declares blessed in 5:7-10 are those
who help to bring to reality the blessings promised to others in
5:3-6.[49]

The *merciful* (*eleēmones*, 5:7; compare Heb 2:17) are those who
exhibit the divine quality of mercy (*eleos*). According to Matthew's Gospel, mercy is one of the weightier matters of the law
(23:23). God desires mercy over sacrifice (9:13; 12:7), and Jesus is
frequently portrayed as responding to the pleas of those who ask
him to have mercy (*eleeō*) on them (9:27; 15:22; 17:15; 20:30, 31).

Many commentators identify mercy in 5:7 with the forgiveness of sins which is to be practiced within communities of
faith.[50] Thus, Matthew's fifth beatitude may be taken as expressing positively the same thought that is expressed negatively in 7:1
("Do not judge, so that you may not be judged"). Such an interpretation draws some support from Jesus' words to the religious
leaders in 9:13 and 12:7, which imply that if they understood
God's preference for mercy, they would not be so quick to judge
others. It is also thought to be illustrated parabolically in 18:23-

---

49. This seems a more logical construal than Hagner's suggestion that the
latter beatitudes describe the demeanor of the needy persons in their unfortunate circumstances (*Matthew 1–13*, 91), so that "what the poor and oppressed
have not received from the rich and powerful, they should nevertheless show
others" (p. 93).

50. Dupont, 3:632–33; Guelich, 88–89; Hamm, 96–99; Kingsbury, *Matthew
as Story*, 132; Schniewind, 46; Soiron, 179–80.

34, where the servant who is forgiven greatly by his king is unable to show mercy (18:33) on a fellow servant by forgiving him even a little. But the real point of these passages goes deeper. What the religious leaders fail to understand is that a merciful God is not pleased by religion that prevents people from eating with outcasts (9:10-13) or, for that matter, from eating, period (12:1-7). And although the cancellation of debt in 18:33 certainly symbolizes forgiveness of sins (18:21-22), we should not pass too quickly over the immediate, literal sense—economic relief (6:12).[51] Elsewhere in Matthew, a cognate of the word for mercy (*eleēmosynē*) is used to describe the practice of giving money to the poor (6:2, 3, 4). Thus, many scholars insist on a broader application for "being merciful," one that encompasses deeds of loving kindness and acts of compassion in addition to forgiveness of sins.[52]

Several times in Matthew "to show mercy" means to heal those who are sick (9:27; 20:30, 31) or possessed by demons (15:22; 17:17). As such, acts of mercy may represent instances in which the rule of God comes upon people and the house of Satan is plundered (12:28-29). Notably, when eating with outcasts is presented as an example of being merciful in 9:10-13, Jesus describes this activity metaphorically as being a physician to "those who are sick" (9:12). In a basic sense, then, "the merciful" (5:7) are healers, people who seek to put right that which has gone wrong. They favor the removal of everything that prevents life from being as God intends: poverty, ostracism, hunger, disease, demons, debt.

Such a broadened understanding of mercy implies that it is not just a virtue to be practiced within the religious community. Indeed, Matthew's Gospel emphasizes that mercy is to be shown to outcasts (9:10-13) and foreigners (15:21-28). If anything, the fear is that attention to matters important within the community will supersede concern for mercy (23:23; compare 9:10-13; 12:1-7).

The blessing pronounced on the merciful is that they will receive mercy. Surely this means that they themselves will be

51. Crosby, 189–90.
52. Davies and Allison, 454–55; Gundry, 70–71; Luz, 238; and Strecker, 39.

treated with mercy on the final day of judgment, but in a broader sense it may mean simply that they will see mercy prevail. They will receive mercy not only for themselves but also for those on whose behalf they have sought it. The advent of God's kingdom is a blessing to those who value mercy, because God also values mercy and, when God rules, what God values will become reality. The reference to the *pure in heart* (5:8) is a general description of virtuous people that should not be defined with too much precision. Homiletical treatments that speak of people with "clean thoughts" or even Kierkegaard's famous dictum regarding those who "will one thing"[53] limit the range of application for this expression. The heart (*kardia*) cannot be linked definitively with any one sphere of human activity such as cognition or volition. According to Matthew's Gospel, the heart is the source of outward speech (12:34; 15:18) and behavior (15:19) as well as the realm of inner reflection (9:4; 24:48). That which is associated with the heart is not intrinsically good or evil: people lust in their hearts (5:27-28) and love with their hearts (22:37). Here and elsewhere in the Bible *kardia* seems simply to represent "the true self," what one really is apart from pretense. Thus, to "understand with the heart" (13:15) means to understand truly; to "forgive from the heart" (18:35) means to forgive truly; and so on.

The concept of purity, of course, has its background in Old Testament codes that define what is and is not pleasing to God. In Matthew's Gospel, the concern for ritual or cultic purity is not entirely absent (8:2-4) but tends to be transcended or redefined in moral terms (15:10-20; 23:25). What remains, however, is the general understanding of purity as the absence of corruption. A dish (23:26) or a linen (27:59) is *katharos* ("clean" or "pure") when it is free of contamination. Likewise, people must be "made clean" (*katharizō*) in a cultic sense when they have leprosy (8:2, 3; 10:8; 11:5) or in a moral sense when they are "full of greed and self-indulgence" (23:25). To be "pure in heart," then, may mean to have a heart that does not produce those things that defile: evil intentions, murder, adultery, fornication, theft, false

---

53. Søren Kierkegaard, *Purity of Heart Is to Will One Thing: Spiritual Preparation for the Feast of Confession*, trans. D. V. Steere (New York: Harper & Brothers, 1938).

witness, slander (15:19). Or it may mean simply to have a heart that has not "grown dull" to God's word (13:15). And, although the intrinsic sense of *katharos* may be an absence of negative features, this would seem to imply a potential for positive ones. The heart that has not grown dull is open to understanding God's word (13:15), and the heart that does not produce words that condemn may produce words that justify (12:37). So, without too great a stretch we could find many more examples of the pure in heart: those who store up treasure in heaven so that their hearts will be there also (6:21); those who bear fruit because their hearts provide good soil for the word of the kingdom (13:23; compare 13:19); those who love the Lord God with all their hearts and their neighbors as themselves (22:37-39); and so on.

Since the expression has such a wide range of application, we must zero in on the main point of its usage in Matthew's Gospel. From what was said of *kardia* above, we may surmise that the pure in heart are those who are *truly* pure as opposed to those who are only apparently so (23:25-28). Just as people may worship God with their lips when their hearts are far from God (15:8), so also may they appear *katharos* to others when they are actually full of *akatharsia* ("uncleanness," 23:28). Thus, many commentators believe the real accent in Matthew's sixth beatitude is on integrity.[54] This appears also to be the sense in Psalm 24:4, where the pure in heart are contrasted with those given to falsehood or deceit (compare Gen 20:5-6).

Purity of heart, then, is too all-encompassing a concept to be limited to expressions of inward piety or to virtues displayed within the community. If anything, the context of Matthew's other beatitudes shifts the focus to an integrity of virtue that is displayed on behalf of others. Taken in isolation, the verse may pronounce a blessing on any whose virtue is genuine and uncorrupted; in context, the blessing is primarily for those who, with integrity, exhibit such virtues as showing mercy (5:7) and making peace (5:9). Indeed, only those who possess such an integrity will be willing to suffer persecution in order to see right prevail (5:10).

54. Davies and Allison, 456; Guelich, 90–91; Hagner, *Matthew 1–13*, 94; and Luz, 238–39.

The blessing pronounced on the pure in heart is that they will "see God." Since even Moses is unable to see God in this life (Exod 33:20; compare 19:21) this promise surely refers to the end of time when the righteous will be welcomed into the kingdom of their father where they will shine like the sun (13:43; 25:34) and, presumably, enjoy the intimacy of God's presence in a sense that is not possible here. Such a blessing is especially appropriate for the pure in heart because, as people who are truly pleasing to God, they have offered the world a vision of what is godly. Those who will see God are those in whom something of God has been seen.

The beatitude for *the peacemakers* (5:9) is also interpreted in ways that are too limited.[55] First, the term may be taken as a reference to those who bring others to peace with God. Such an application should not be ruled out altogether, but, in general, biblical references to seeking or making peace envision the sphere of human relations (Ps 34:14; Prov 10:10; Mark 9:50; Jas 3:18; but see Col 1:20). More often, Matthew 5:9 is thought to refer to those who work for reconciliation within the community of faith. Thus, examples of peacemakers in Matthew's Gospel would include a person who leaves a gift at the altar to seek reconciliation with another community member (5:23-24) and people who respond to a sinful member of the community in the way described by Jesus in 18:15-18. Such reconciliation implies a generosity of forgiveness (18:21-35), and so this understanding of peacemakers is congruent with interpretations that take "the merciful" in 5:7 to be those who exercise forgiveness within the community. A somewhat broader paradigm identifies peacemakers also with those who seek reconciliation with the world at large.[56] Under this interpretation, examples of peacemakers would also include those who come to terms quickly with their

55. But then Davies and Allison (p. 458) remind us with a smile that Origen included those who reconcile contradictory biblical texts among the "peacemakers."

56. Dupont, 3:635–40; Dieter Lührmann, "Liebet eure Feinde (Lk 6, 27–36/Mt 5, 39–48)," *ZTK* 69 (1972): 412–38; and Luz, 241. Direct application to elimination of war between nations (Davies and Allison, 458) or to nonviolent revolution (Hagner, *Matthew 1–13*, 94) does not appear to be primary, although neither should be excluded from the possible range of meaning.

accusers (5:25) and, especially, those who love their enemies (5:44). The latter application is appealing because Jesus describes those who love their enemies as "children of the Father in heaven," a phrase that recalls the apodosis of this beatitude. Any interpretation that equates peacemaking with reconciliation, however, fails to take into account Jesus' claim that he has not come to bring peace in this sense of the word (10:34). The expectation, in fact, is that association with him will create divisions and evoke hostility (10:35-36; compare 5:11-12; 10:21-22).

Although the word *eirēnopoioi* is not used elsewhere in the New Testament, it does occur in Greco-Roman literature where it applies to rulers who establish security and socioeconomic welfare.[57] We may assume that this sense of the term would be intensified in a Semitic document such as Matthew's Gospel because of the influence of the Hebrew concept of *shalom*, which is typically translated by *eirēnē* ("peace") in the LXX. Reconciliation of the estranged would be one example of *shalom*, but this is certainly not the exclusive or even primary application of the term. In the Old Testament, *shalom* is a parallel term for *mishpat* ("justice"), such that peace "is not seen as tranquility and order, but rather as the deep commitment to the work of justice."[58] The peacemakers whom Jesus pronounces blessed in 5:9 are best regarded as agents of God who are actively establishing *shalom*.[59] Or, as Jack Kingsbury says, they are "those who work for the wholeness and well-being that God wills for a broken world."[60]

The blessing attributed to these people is that they will be called children of God. In Matthew's Gospel, people are identified as God's children when their conduct is similar to God's own (5:48), in the same way that people are identified as members of Jesus' family when they do God's will (12:50). The assumption seems to be that for those involved in bringing about what God wants, the acknowledgment that they have behaved as God's children and done as God wished will be reward enough.

---

57. See Hans Windisch, "Friedensbringer—Gottessohn," *ZNW* 24 (1925): 240–60; esp. 240–41.

58. *ABD*, 5:206.

59. Guelich, 91–92; Hamm, 102–6; Meier, *Matthew*, 41–42; Schniewind, 48; and Windisch, "Friedensbringer."

60. Kingsbury, *Matthew as Story*, 133.

In the blessing on *those who are persecuted for the sake of righteousness/justice* (5:10), the word *dikaiosynē* is used with a different sense than it was in 5:6.[61] As we have seen, true righteousness or justice is something that must ultimately be established by God, but people are invited to repent and participate now in that establishment (3:2; 4:17). Such participation brings persecution. The virtue commended here is not persecution itself but the degree of investment that may be assumed for those so committed to God's cause that they are willing to suffer for it. Such people may be contrasted with those who receive the word of the kingdom with joy but immediately fall away when tribulation or persecution arises on account of the word (13:20-21).

This eighth beatitude serves as a fitting conclusion to the second stanza of four and summarizes the basic thought of the unit. Those who show mercy and those who work to establish God's *shalom* are examples of people committed to *dikaiosynē*, and if these people are pure in heart, then their commitment will not falter in the face of persecution. In every case, the people described by these beatitudes are virtuous. They display qualities that, ideally, all people should display. In one sense, then, the thought of the second set of beatitudes is quite different from that of the first. When God's kingdom comes and God's will is done, no one will have to be poor in spirit, mourn, be meek, or hunger and thirst for righteousness/justice, but everyone who is ruled by God and does God's will is merciful, pure in heart, committed to peacemaking, and willing to suffer for the sake of righteousness/justice.

Relationship of the Two Stanzas. In the discussion above we have noted that two distinct patterns of parallelism may be detected for Matthew 5:3-6 and Matthew 5:7-10. These patterns establish an internal integrity for each of these units that allows them to be recognized as separate stanzas. At the same time, a number of features enable us to identify structural, logical, and theological connections between the two stanzas.

---

61. Most scholars grant that in 5:10, *dikaiosynē* refers to behavior in keeping with God's will. See, e.g., Davies and Allison, 459–60; Guelich, 93; Kingsbury, *Matthew as Story*, 133; and Luz, 242.

The primary structural connection is established by the apodosis of the eighth beatitude (5:10b), which repeats verbatim that
of the first (5:3b). This rhetorical *inclusio* suggests that everything
from 5:3 through 5:10 is to be read as a single unit. The protosis
of the eighth beatitude, furthermore, picks up the concern for
dikaiosynē in 5:6. This repetition suggests that these two verses
function analogously, as the concluding lines of stanzas that
belong to the same poem.

Indications of structural unity encourage readers to look for a
logical relationship between the connected passages. Here, that
relationship is seen in the concern for *dikaiosynē* evident in both
stanzas. Whereas the first stanza deals with those who have been
deprived of righteousness/justice (5:6), the second is concerned
with those dedicated to the establishment of righteousness/
justice (5:10). Thus, the people described in the second stanza
supply what those described in the first stanza lack.

On another level, however, the connection between these two
stanzas transcends logic with an ironic realization that belongs to
Matthew's eschatological vision. Although Matthew's text offers
no support for regarding the unfortunate in 5:3-6 as "a little bit
virtuous," it does indicate through the mention of persecution
(5:10) that the virtuous people described in 5:7-10 are in some
sense unfortunate. The misfortune that they suffer, furthermore,
comes as a direct result of their commitment to bringing
righteousness/justice to the unfortunate ones who hunger and
thirst for it. The ironic connection between the stanzas, then, lies
in the realization that those who practice the virtues described in
the second stanza may on that account come to be numbered
among those described in the first stanza on whose behalf these
virtues are exercised. This ironic identification of the virtuous
with the unfortunate is consistent with Matthew's projection of
the rule of God evidenced by Jesus. Drawing on the "suffering
servant" theme of Isaiah, Matthew presents Jesus as one who
seeks to proclaim justice to those who have been deprived of it
and who, accordingly, comes to be deprived of it himself (12:18-
21; compare Isa 42:1-4). Thus, Jesus is the king who becomes
praüs ("meek" or "oppressed," 21:5), the lord who becomes a
servant (20:28). Being *praüs* is not a virtue in and of itself, but
becoming *praüs* voluntarily for the sake of others is. In this sense,
the second stanza of the beatitudes describes behavior that is

deemed virtuous because it is exercised on behalf of the unfortunate and that is deemed all the more virtuous when it involves voluntary identification with the unfortunate. Such ironic logic is consistent with Jesus' description of children as "humble" (a condition, not a virtue)[62] and encouragement for his disciples to change and "become humble" (*tapeineō*) like children (18:1-4). A theological link between the stanzas can be seen in the content of the blessings that are promised. The blessings of the first stanza may be construed as reversals and those of the second as rewards, but in either case these blessings represent the intrinsic effects of God's rule being established. Whether the coming of God's kingdom is perceived as bringing reversal or reward depends only on the position that one occupies prior to its advent. God's rule sets things right. Those for whom things have not been right are blessed by the changes it brings and those who have been seeking to set things right are blessed by the accomplishment of what they have sought.

Concluding Comment (5:11-12). After the eight beatitudes that constitute a two-stanza poem, Jesus utters a final, ninth beatitude addressed to his disciples. This beatitude expands upon the last verse of the second stanza, offering a conditional application of that blessing to the disciples themselves. But since, as we have noted, Matthew 5:10 serves as a summation of 5:7-9 and is also linked to 5:3 and 5:6, the effect of Jesus' concluding comment is to offer his disciples the possibility of identification with those described in all of the preceding beatitudes. This comes as a revelation, because nothing in Matthew's narrative up to now has indicated that Jesus' disciples suffer the misfortunes of those described in 5:3-6 or exhibit the virtues of those described in 5:7-10. But when they are reviled, persecuted, and slandered on account of Jesus, they will find themselves among those who are ironically deprived of justice because of their devotion to it.

62. Children are identified as humble not because they are perceived as modest or self-effacing but because they are regarded as "the weakest, most vulnerable members of society." Bruce J. Malina and Richard L. Rohrbaugh, *Social-Science Commentary on the Synoptic Gospels* (Minneapolis: Fortress Press, 1992), 117.

Although this concluding comment is the only beatitude addressed to the disciples in the second person, the disciples are presented as the immediate audience for all of the beatitudes (5:1-2). The effect of the earlier third-person narration is twofold. First, it establishes the blessed as a field of persons larger than the disciples of Jesus (compare the reference to "the prophets who were before you" in 5:12). Jesus' disciples may come to be numbered among the blessed, but they are not identical with them. Second, it creates an initial distance that allows Jesus' audience to hear his words impartially before realizing the direct application to themselves. Such distance is rhetorically effective in that it creates an illusion of safety that falls away after the essential point has been made. Such tactics are necessary because of the paradoxical quality of the blessings Jesus wishes to attribute to his disciples. Although we might assume that anyone would want to be called "blessed," we cannot assume that everyone would want to be included among the categories of blessed persons delineated here.

In literary terms, the disciples of Jesus function as the *narratee* for the beatitudes in Matthew's Gospel. The specification of a narratee for discourse indicates the perspective from which the readers are expected to hear what is said. In actual circumstances, empathy of readers is impossible to predict. Readers who consider themselves to be unfortunate might immediately identify with the characters described in Matthew 5:3-6, or those who consider themselves to be virtuous might do the same with the characters described in 5:7-10. But specification of the disciples as the explicit narratee for Jesus' words indicates that Matthew's *implied* readers are expected to identify with them and to evaluate what Jesus says from their perspective.[63]

When the beatitudes are read from this perspective, the sudden shift to the second person in 5:11 assaults Matthew's readers in the world outside the story as surely as it does the disciples within the story. Until now, the readers have been learning, along with the disciples, that the coming of God's kingdom brings blessing to the unfortunate people of the earth and to

63. On the notion of narratees and implied readers, see Powell, *Narrative Criticism*, 19–21, 27.

those virtuous ones who work and even suffer on their behalf. Then, suddenly, the disciples are told that their commitment to Jesus means that they will be numbered among the suffering virtuous ones and thus, in some sense, among the unfortunate ones as well. At this point in the narrative, Matthew's readers are expected to realize that continued empathy with the disciples means adopting a perspective that leads to identification with those whom Jesus has declared blessed. The empathy that has already been established between Matthew's readers and the disciples encourages such identification.

In recognition that some readers may be resistant, Matthew's Gospel offers another possibility for empathy. When Jesus finishes the discourse that begins with the beatitudes, we are told that "the crowds were astounded at his teaching" (7:28). This is surprising information, because we have previously been led to believe that Jesus was speaking to his disciples apart from the crowds (5:1-2). With the realization that the crowds have overheard what Jesus said, Matthew's readers are offered, belatedly, a second narratee—an alternative point of view from which the words of Jesus may also be heard. Presumably, this point of view will be an option for those readers who have been unable to adopt the perspective of the disciples, the perspective from which they were encouraged to hear Jesus' words. Readers who have heard the words from the disciples' point of view are left at the end of Jesus' speech with only two options: act or don't act (7:24-27). Readers who have not been able to hear the words from this perspective are expected to identify instead with the crowds to whom the words were not really addressed in the first place. Their experience will be that of outsiders, eavesdropping on communication that evinces an authority unknown to them. Rather than feeling compelled to decide whether or not to act, they will be simply "astounded" (7:28-29). Perhaps on a subsequent reading, such readers will be able to accept Matthew's initial invitation to hear the words as disciples addressed by Jesus rather than just as crowds who overhear what is said to others.

SALT AND LIGHT

The preceding analysis challenges the widely held notion that Matthew's Gospel is interested only in justice practiced within the community of faith rather than in justice enacted by the community within the world at large. If the interpretation seems unconvincing, however, we need look only to the next few verses of Matthew's Gospel for corroboration. Jesus describes his disciples as "the salt of the earth" (5:13) and "the light of the world" (5:14). While the exact meaning of these metaphors is open to discussion,[64] an indisputable point would be that the presence of Jesus' disciples makes the world a better place than it would be without them. Their community is not only to provide a refuge from the injustice of the world but is also to remain actively involved in the world through the performance of good works (5:16). Indeed, disciples of Jesus who do not do good works for the world are as worthless as salt that is not salty or light that cannot be seen. In other words, the very purpose of their existence is not being fulfilled.

Since Matthew does not specify here what is meant by "good works," we ought to take the expression as a generic reference that might include acts of charity,[65] obedience to the law,[66] and other possibilities. Two applications for the term, however, are especially attractive. First, immediate context suggests that the virtues just mentioned in the beatitudes are prime examples of the good works that fulfill the disciples' role as salt and light. Second, the good works expected of Jesus' followers ought to be defined with reference to the activity of Jesus himself. Matthew's Gospel prepares its readers for such a connection by referring to Jesus as "a light" just a few verses prior to this passage (4:16). As the story progresses, an act of healing performed by Jesus will be explicitly identified as a good work (12:15), and such actions will indeed lead people to glorify God (9:8; 15:31).

These two applications are complementary, for both suggest enactments of justice on behalf of the unfortunate. As we have seen, the second stanza of the beatitudes refers to persons committed to bringing the righteousness/justice (*dikaiosynē*) of God to those who are described in the first stanza as deprived of it.

64. To survey options, see Davies and Allison, 472–75; Guelich, 126–28; and Luz, 248–52.

65. Gundry, 78.

66. Or, specifically, to the commands of Jesus that fulfill the law (5:17). Davies and Allison, 479.

Similarly, the healing ministry of Jesus is what identifies him as one who proclaims justice (*krisis*) to the Gentiles (12:15-18). Indeed, healing is one way of showing mercy (9:27; 15:22; 17:17; 20:30, 31) and also one way of making peace (in the sense of establishing *shalom*). The basic point is that the good works that mark Jesus' followers as the salt of the earth and the light of the world are acts that put God's rule into effect by setting things right. Showing mercy, making peace, healing the sick, and exorcising demons exemplify such acts without exhausting the possibilities. In every case, these acts are performed for the benefit of the unfortunate people of the world for whom things are not as God wants them to be.

The relationship of this text to Matthew's notion of social justice is often missed by interpretations that view the main concern of 5:13-16 as evangelistic. Since Jesus says those who see his disciples' good works will give glory to the Father in heaven (5:16), these works may be viewed as enticements to conversion. A variation on this view allows that the church's task may be exemplary as well as evangelistic. Thus, one commentator suggests that the followers of Jesus are "to be detached from the world, and yet their very existence is such that they cannot but exercise an influence on that world."[67] According to this interpretation, we ought to beware of using this passage "as a kind of proof text of the often-expressed homiletic concern for 'involvement.' "[68]

These interpretations miss the point not only of this passage but of the eschatological mission of the church described in Matthew's Gospel as a whole. A supposed exemplary role for the church may be discounted immediately because Matthew's Gospel betrays no notion that the world will ever improve based on what it learns from Jesus' followers. In fact, the latter will be hated by all nations (24:9), and the situation of the world in general will get worse, not better, before the end (24:21). Ironically, the emphasis on the evangelistic role of the church draws its strength precisely from this recognition. The thought is that, since the church will never transform society, its contribution to social justice must be to offer an alternative society, one in which

67. Albright and Mann, 55.
68. Ibid.

the justice that is not found in the world is practiced. But there is another possibility. In addition to practicing justice within its own community, the church may be called to perform justice in a society that itself remains untransformed. Just as Jesus viewed his role as being to plunder the house of the devil (12:28-29), so his followers might enact the justice of God in a world that views them as unwelcome intruders. Such a role is consistent with the charter for the church provided in Matthew 16:18 (overcoming the gates of Hades) and with Jesus' commission to his disciples to proclaim the imminence of God's rule by healing the sick, raising the dead, cleansing lepers, and casting out demons (10:7-8). Active engagement or "involvement" with the world is assumed.

Matthew's Gospel is certainly interested in evangelism, but we must question whether that is a primary focus of Matthew 5:13-16. For one thing, giving glory to the Father in heaven (5:16) cannot be equated with conversion. Elsewhere in Matthew, people glorify God in response to what Jesus does (9:8; 15:31), but none of those who do so are described as taking up his cause or becoming his disciples.[69] Jesus never performs any works intended to attract disciples and, in fact, refuses to offer signs to those who look for them (12:38-39; 16:1-4). Jesus heals sick people not so that they will follow him but because he is the agent of God and God does not want people to be sick. Beyond this, the only personal motivation for such activity ascribed to Jesus is compassion (9:36; 14:14; 15:32; 20:34),[70] a trait that is also parabolically attributed to God (18:27). The objects of Jesus' compassion range from those who are with him (15:32) to those who seek his mercy (20:30-34) to great throngs of the "harassed and helpless" (9:36; 14:14).

According to Matthew's Gospel, then, God cares about the welfare of all people, not just those who belong to the appropriate religious community. The imminence of God's kingdom implies the dawn of an age in which God's will is done. Jesus and his followers participate in this new age by performing good works that set things right. Many people, especially the unfortunate,

---

69. The point of 5:16b is probably that the disciples ought to do good works that bring glory to the Father *rather than* to themselves (6:1-2).

70. In 9:6, the healing of the paralytic is not presented as an evangelistic ploy but as a demonstration of the role of God imminent in Jesus' own ministry.

will be blessed by such activity and will glorify God in response
to it, but this does not necessarily mean that they will repent,
obey God's law, be baptized, join the church, or make any other
religious commitment. It certainly does not mean that the good
works performed by Jesus and his followers are done in order to
provoke such commitments. Jesus' followers are called to make
disciples of all nations (28:19), but they are also called to do good
works that have an integrity of their own.

CONCLUSION

Matthew's concept of social justice must be understood in light
of the Gospel's eschatological perspective. According to Matthew's vision, the world has in large measure fallen under the
control of the devil (4:8-9). Recognition of this state of affairs is
sufficient for understanding why things are not as they ought to
be, as God would desire for them to be. But now, God's rule has
come near (3:2; 4:17; 10:7)—already present in the activity of
Jesus and his followers and soon to be established in its fullness at
the close of the age.

Given this perspective, the church realizes, on the one hand,
that true righteousness/justice can be established only by God
through a cosmic reordering of heaven and earth (24:29-31). The
world will not be a just place until the devil and his minions have
been removed, cast into the fires prepared for them (13:40-42;
25:41). The church expects this to happen soon but knows that in
the meantime the world will only get worse (24:21). The church
will not transform society.

But this is not the whole story. According to Matthew's
Gospel, the kingdom of heaven has come so near that the effects
of its approach are already being realized. Even now, the house of
Satan can be plundered (12:29) and the forces of disease, death,
uncleanness, and demons can be overcome (10:8). Because this is
true, Jesus and his followers are able to enact the justice of God
even before that time when God transforms the world itself. The
church is less a fortress than an army, assaulting the very gates of
Hades which cannot prevail against it (16:18).

In short, everything will be put right by God at the close of the
age, but some things can be put right by God's agents even now.
If we ask which particular aspects of God's rule the church is to

enact in the present world, Matthew's Gospel suggests numerous possibilities. The beatitudes prioritize reversal of conditions for the unfortunate, including those who have no reason for hope or cause for joy, who have been deprived of their share of the earth's bounty and of justice in general. Such people may be helped even now by those whose purity of heart and commitment to establishing mercy, peace, and justice is so great that they are willing to suffer for it. The story of Jesus' own ministry highlights concern for those afflicted by disease and demons, and these may also be helped by followers of Jesus whose good works make them salt for the earth and light for the world.

As we have indicated, however, the expressions and metaphors that Matthew's Gospel employs for social justice are generic ones that might encompass a wide range of meaning. Showing mercy, for example, may refer to forgiveness (18:33) or to healing (9:27; 15:22; 17:15; 20:30, 31).[71] By the same token, healings and exorcisms exemplify good works that cause people to glorify God (12:15; compare 9:8; 15:31) but they do not exhaust the possible meaning of the "light of the world" metaphor. The ambiguity of such terms must be preserved, for Matthew's Gospel is more interested in establishing the church's mandate to work for God's righteousness/justice in the world than in defining the specific agenda that the church is to follow in doing so.

This chapter has concentrated on affirming the commitment of Matthew's Gospel to that mandate in defiance of much contemporary scholarship to the contrary. We have examined only a few key verses, but the hope is that further reflection on the whole of Matthew's Gospel may now proceed unencumbered by assumptions that predispose interpreters to look only for that which addresses justice practiced within the community.[72] To take but two examples, we might call for further reflection on Matthew 20:25-26 and on Matthew 25:31-46, texts mentioned in the first paragraphs of this chapter.

71. The two concepts are not far removed, as Matthew 9:6 indicates.

72. Nlenanya Onwu lists six social implications inherent in Matthew's concept of righteousness/justice: affirmation of the worth of human life, protection of human rights, new patterns of social relationships, redistribution of wealth, political participation, and fulfillment of civic responsibility. See "Righteousness in Matthew's Gospel: Its Social Implications," *Bhy* 13 (1987): 151–78.

Jesus acknowledges in 20:25-26 that the world's political rulers do not practice the sort of justice that he expects to be practiced among his followers. But does this necessarily mean that the church should be content to establish communities that provide refuge from the injustice of the world without directly challenging the world's unjust authorities? John the Baptist, who Jesus says "came in the way of righteousness/justice" (21:32), opposes Herod the tetrarch in Matthew's Gospel (14:3-4). Jesus attacks religious authorities who make the temple a den of robbers (21:12-13) and burden others without offering to help (23:4). Jesus' followers will be killed, crucified, scourged, and persecuted by these religious leaders (23:34), and they will be dragged before governors and kings to bear testimony (10:18). Far from endorsing a passive role by which the church limits its contribution to social justice to the construction of alternative societies, Matthew's Gospel presents an expectation that Jesus' followers will be engaged in direct confrontation with the world's most powerful exponents of injustice. In this and in any number of other ways, the church is envisioned as not only striving to bring people into a community committed to practicing God's justice but also as acting for justice in the unconverted world that persecutes them for doing so.

As we have already noted, the primary concern in Matthew 25:31-46 is not with acts of mercy performed *by* church members for needy people of the world but with acts of mercy performed *for* church members by people among the nations to which they are sent.[73] But the passage develops the latter theme as a corol-

73. Scholars who acknowledge that this is so but wish to redeem the text for contemporary discussions of social ethics often adopt one or more of the following strategies: (*a*) ascribe the sectarian tendencies of the current text to Matthean redaction and posit an original version that did endorse universal charity. Johannes Friedrich, *Gott im Bruder? Eine methodenkritische Untersuchung von Redaktion, Überlieferung, und Traditionen in Mt 25, 31-46* (Stuttgart: Calwer Verlag, 1977); and Jan Lambrecht, *Once More Astonished: The Parables of Jesus* (New York: Crossroad, 1981), 211–35; (*b*) suggest that a comparative rhetorical ploy is operative, as in 5:43-48 (if even pagans are to do deeds of mercy, how much more Christian disciples?). John R. Donahue, "The 'Parable' of the Sheep and the Goats: A Challenge to Christian Ethics," *TS* 47 (1986): 3–31, esp. 28; and Daniel J. Harrington, *The Gospel of Matthew* (SP; Collegeville, Minn.: Liturgical Press, 1991), 360; and (*c*) argue that the apocalyptic or para-

lary to the former, which is established earlier in Matthew. Matthew's Gospel leaves no doubt that followers of Jesus are to meet needs of people outside the community of faith. Their good works are to enlighten the *world* (5:13-16). They are to love even their *enemies* (5:44). They are to emulate their heavenly Father who provides for the *evil* and the *unrighteous* as surely as for the good and the righteous (5:45). Indeed, Matthew notes with some irony that what makes true children of the Father different from others is, specifically, their commitment to others (5:47). Followers of Jesus, furthermore, will be held accountable for their faithfulness in these matters. Those who call him "Lord" will enter the kingdom of heaven only if they do the will of the Father (7:21), which certainly includes being light for the world, loving their enemies, and in other ways demonstrating commitment to justice for those outside the community of faith.

All of these points are made in Jesus' first great discourse in Matthew's Gospel and are expected to make an early impression on Matthew's readers. Matthew 25:31-46 comes at the very end of Jesus' final great discourse and offers a turnabout that completes the picture.[74] Now the readers are told that the world (the nations)[75] will also be held accountable for its treatment of Jesus' followers. The fact that many real readers miss this turnabout and simply assume that the passage addresses the necessity of Christian charity confirms that the turnabout is unexpected. Although such a reading may be based on a less careful analysis than would be attributed to Matthew's ideal or implied reader, it is nevertheless understandable, for the perspective this passage offers is different from that with which readers have become accustomed. That followers of Jesus ought to do unto others as they would have done to them (7:12) is a major theme in Matthew. The corollary to this—that others ought to treat the fol-

---

bolic character of the text discourages identification of either the givers or recipients of mercy. Donahue, " 'Parable,' " 11.

74. Similar points have been made earlier but with specific reference to Israel's response to Jesus' disciples (10:5, 14-15, 40-42).

75. Some interpreters take *ethnē* ("nations") in 25:32 as referring specifically to (non-Christian) Gentiles, under the assumption that the church is here regarded as the true Israel. See Douglas R. A. Hare, *Matthew* (Interpretation Series; Louisville: John Knox Press, 1993), 288–91; and Harrington, 355–60.

lowers of Jesus as they themselves would wish to be treated—is of course also true but is seldom expressed (but see 10:14-15, 40-42). Thus, even though Matthew 25:31-46 does not express the divine expectation that the church should be involved in working for justice in the world as explicitly as is sometimes thought, the passage may be said to *assume* such an expectation and to offer insight that builds upon it. The siblings of Jesus whom the nations have assisted or ignored are themselves described twice in this passage as "just" (*dikaios*, 25:37, 46)[76], that is, as persons who have suffered gladly in order to bring justice to those who are deprived of it (5:6, 11-12).

76. Donahue, " 'Parable,' " 22.

INDEX OF
MATTHEAN PASSAGES

INDEX OF
MODERN AUTHORS